IMAGES
of America

DICKENSON
COUNTY

IMAGES
of America

DICKENSON
COUNTY

Victoria L. Osborne

ARCADIA
PUBLISHING

Published by Arcadia Publishing
Charleston, South Carolina

Library of Congress Catalog Card Number: 2006935463

For all general information contact Arcadia Publishing at:
Telephone 843-853-2070
Fax 843-853-0044
E-mail sales@arcadiapublishing.com
For customer service and orders:
Toll-Free 1-888-313-2665

Visit us on the Internet at www.arcadiapublishing.com

CONTENTS

ACKNOWLEDGMENTS

Dennis Reedy of Clinchco, Virginia, is owed a great debt of thanks for his efforts to preserve the history of Southwest Virginia. Thanks go to Aaron Davies of the Ralph Stanley Museum and Norma Morris, publicist for Ralph Stanley. Ralph Stanley is thanked for his insight into Dickenson County. Thanks also go to the Dickenson County Library for its help in the history of the county, the Washington County Historical Society, and the Southwest Virginia Historical and Preservation Society for opening its archives. I also wish to thank my editor, Courtney Hutton, for her tireless assistance.

FOREWORD

When one thinks of Dickenson County they think of Virginia's baby county. I think of it as home. I've traveled throughout the United States, visiting all 50 states and 14 countries. But all pale in comparison to my home in Dickenson County. I always look forward to returning to my home, and it never disappoints me. For me growing up in Dickenson was a fun-filled time with my friends and brother, Carter. We would often attend the trials of the day and listen to the lawyers argue their cases and Judge Galley Friend make his rulings. Our lives were filled with family and neighbors, a life where respect of God and family governed our every action. The greatest influence in my life was my mother, who had a faith in our music and encouraged Carter and myself to pursue that gift to make it a reality. I modeled my style in the early days after Bill Monroe and the Carter Family. Later my own style emerged. We often played at the Morgan Theatre that is now the Jettie Baker Center, and I fondly remember those as the good old days. This year and this month of October 2006 makes my 60th year in the music business, and I have had the pleasure of seeing the musical legacy continue in my son and grandson. Dr. Osborne shows the reader in this Images of America series that the way of life in Dickenson County was hard but filled with love and respect of God and family, with an appreciation of the gifts that God gave us.

—Dr. Ralph Stanley

INTRODUCTION

Dickenson County was formed in 1880 from parts of Wise, Russell, and Buchanan Counties. The county was named for William J. Dickenson, a state legislator from Russell County who was the patron for the bill in the house of delegates in 1880 to establish Dickenson as the 100th county in Virginia. Dickenson would be forever known as Virginia's baby county.

Some of the senate members wanted to name the county "Stonewall" in honor of Gen. Stonewall Jackson. The bill was approved by Gov. Frederick W. M. Holliday. The county seat was first located near the mouth of Caney Fork on the McClure River. It was named Ervinton in honor of Micajah Ervin, one of the early settlers. The first circuit court was held on May 30, 1881, with Judge John A. Kelly presiding. The courthouse was rebuilt in 1884 and remodeled in 1915–1916, and it contained fireproof vaults for the clerk and treasurer.

Daniel Boone may have been one of the earliest white settlers. In the autumn of 1767, he and two others traveled northward from their homes on the Yadkin River in North Carolina and reached the headwaters of the West (later called Russell) Fork of the Big Sandy River. The first hunters found Dickenson a paradise. Hunters would make camp, hunt, and prepare skins for many months before returning to their homes; thus they became known as the Long Hunters. Richard "Fighting Dick" Colley made the first white settlement three miles south of Haysi. Legend has it he killed a black bear with his own hands. In the mid-1700s, John Swift met a man by the name of George Mundy. Mundy had been held captive by Native Americans in the Great Wilderness for about three years before he escaped. Mundy had an extensive knowledge of silver mines, which Swift found interesting. At the mouth of Roaring Fork on the McClure River and south of the mountains, prospectors dug for silver. The mine was located in a large laurel thicket. Three mines were opened, and Swift's company built a furnace for smelting ore. The first venture ended in 1760 a great success. At that point, the groups divided into two teams. One went to Kentucky and the other went southwest. No more silver was ever found. Legend says that silver is still in the Cumberland Mountains.

The only known Revolutionary War soldier buried in Dickenson County rests on a knoll east of McClure and Mullins.

The county's economy has always been dependent upon natural resources—first, game and fur; second, timber; and third; coal. Wash Brittin (or Briton), of Brittin and Pennsylvania Company, began the timber industry around 1867. The first contract for sale of timber was made by A. D. Alley to Horsley and Tate in 1885. The W. M. Ritter Lumber Company bought most of the valuable timber in the county and was a major employer. The first contract recorded for minerals in Dickenson County occurred in 1886 when Richard Hibbitts sold a tract of coal land at 50¢ an acre to G. V. Litchfield. The Steinman Development Company was the first organization of its kind to buy coal deposits in Dickenson County. The Steinmans first purchased 1,000 acres on Cranes Nest River (then in Wise County) from Philip Fleming in December 1874. Times were hard, and every resource was used to supply the everyday needs. Men's everyday clothes were made from flax due to the strength of the material. Homes were built of hewn logs and roofs of boards and dirt or puncheon floors (hewn logs). The people were sociable on the occasions that they had to get together (workings, corn husking, fencings, log rolling, church, and weddings). Quilt gatherings were called workings and were often followed by a party where neighbors could continue to socialize. The day-to-day life was hard and strenuous.

Coal mining began on a large scale in 1916. Clinchfield Coal Corporation was the largest coal producer in Dickenson County. They built one of the county's major towns, Clinchco, around that same year. The Virginia Banner Coal Corporation built the town of Trammel. Splashdam Coal Corporation and Bartlich were built by Bartlich Coal Mining Company. In 1947, Clinchfield Coal opened the Moss No. 1 Preparation Plant and Moss No. 1 Mine. This operation was the largest coal mine in the world at the time. Averaging 200 railroad cars a day, they loaded their one-millionth car on August 11, 1982. In 1979, Clinchfield installed an even larger operation near the county on Caney Creek. This operation was called McClure No. 1 Mine and McClure River Preparation Plant. It was also the largest coal mine in the world for its time. In June 1932, the area suffered a mining tragedy at Splashdam Coal Corporation when an explosion killed 10 men. The probable cause of the explosion was an accumulation of methane gas (firedamp). When the gas, exploded coal dust in the mine was ignited.

The Carolina, Clinchfield, and Ohio Railway was completed in 1915. The last spike was driven at Trammel by the railroad's former president, George L. Carter. Fremont Station was named for John C. Fremont, a renowned western adventurer and explorer known as the "Pathfinder." He was the first Republican candidate to run for the office of president but was defeated by James Buchanan in the 1856 election. Supposedly Fremont was a surveyor on one of the small predecessor lines that eventually became part of Clinchfield. The station was used as a waiting room for passengers and a three-door freight room. By 1919, the freight business had grown so successful that it became necessary to lengthen the freight section by 50 feet, giving three additional doors to each side, and to construct 16 more feet of office space on the north end. The building has remained unchanged since 1919. Before the Fremont station opened, most goods coming into the area were hauled by horse- or mule-drawn wagons from Coeburn, a station on the Norfolk and Western Railway. The station served the businesses in Clintwood, the county stores of the surrounding areas, and the W. M. Ritter Lumber Company operations.

Dickenson County has retained its traditional culture of the Appalachian Mountains. The Breaks Interstate Park was created in 1954 by joint action of the Virginia and Kentucky Legislatures and encompasses 4,500 acres of natural beauty, including the largest canyon east of the Mississippi River at nearly five miles long and 1,600 feet deep.

The first recorded murder in the area occurred in 1817 near Abner's Gap. Sylvanius Brewer, Samuel Endicutt, and others were hunting, and Brewer and Endicutt had an argument over Brewer's wife. Brewer shot and killed Endicutt in the woods and left his body propped against a tree. When Endicutt was missed by others in the party, Brewer claimed not to know what happened. He even joined the search party that found Endicutt. He was arrested, tried, and convicted of the killing. Brewer was hung for the crime.

The first school in Dickenson County was established about 1855 at the mouth of Honey Branch about one and a half miles below Trammel. The first schools were subscription schools, where the teachers were paid a fixed monthly rate (usually $1 or $2) for each pupil. The first school bus was a homemade wooden shed mounted on a 1924 Chevrolet chassis. The bus had wooden seats and a small opening at the back of the door. This bus was owned by W. J. Artrip, who was paid $2.49 a day for its use. Bear Ridge School, in service from 1930 to 1970, was the last log school building to be used in the county.

On June 8, 1948, the town elections in Clintwood, Virginia, drew national and international attention when the voters elected an all-female town council and mayor. Minnie "Sis" Matter was elected mayor. The ladies took office in September 1948. Letters were received from around the world wishing them luck and expressing amazement that an all-woman government could be elected anywhere. The State Department featured the story in its *Voice of America* broadcast. By all accounts, the "Petticoat Government" was highly successful, and during their administration, many important improvement projects were undertaken, including expanding parking in town and installing parking meters in the downtown area. The area has produced a number of famous individuals.

The Bear Pen Dirty Socks baseball team was invited to Kansas to participate in the national semi-pro playoff series. Their record for that year was 23-2. Claude Fuller was nicknamed "Iron Man," a name that was given to him by R. L. Palmer, his boss at the No. 9 Mine in Clinchco. Fuller never missed a shift and would work two shifts a day. He could pitch left-handed and bat right-handed. The Iron Man signed with the New York Yankees for $168 a week and played minor-league ball for six weeks. Congressman John W. Flannagan Jr., "the Clintwood Cyclone," was one of the county's most prominent politicians, representing the "Fighting Ninth" congressional district. The John Flannagan Dam is named for him. The county is home to bluegrass legend Ralph Stanley.

One

BIRTH OF A BABY

DICKENSON COUNTY MARKER. Dickenson County is 335 square miles and includes the Breaks Interstate Park. The county's economy has long been dependent upon natural resources—first, game, second, timber, and third, coal. The first timber industry began around 1867 with a man named Wash Brittin and the Brittin and Pennsylvania Company. The first contract for sale of timber was made by A. D. Alley to Horsley and Tate in 1885. The first deed for poplar trees was made by Almarine Owens to Stephen Bitely in 1887. In 1909, the Yellow Poplar Lumber Company built a concrete splash dam for the purpose of moving logs through the Breaks area. At one time, this structure was the world's largest concrete splash dam. The structure currently supports a highway bridge. Now farming is on a small scale. (Photograph courtesy of the Southwest Virginia Historical and Preservation Society.)

DICKENSON-BUNDY COURTHOUSE. In 1786, Russell County was established. At that time, it represented the areas that are now Lee, Scott, Wise, Dickenson, Buchanan, and Tazewell Counties. This log house, part of which was used in the Dickenson-Bundy Log House, was built on the north side of the Clinch River in 1769 by Henry and Elizabeth Dickenson. (Photograph courtesy of the Southwest Virginia Historical and Preservation Society.)

OLD COURTHOUSE MARKER. The marker shows the site for the Old Russell County Courthouse. The highway marker program was started in Virginia in 1926 to designate historic sites, places, and battles. The original courthouse was built of logs by Henry Dickenson at Dickensonville. It burned during the Revolutionary War. This structure was used as a courthouse until 1818. (Photograph courtesy of the Southwest Virginia Historical and Preservation Society.)

HENRY DICKENSON'S LEGACY. Henry Dickenson had a distinguished beard that made him noticeable from distance. He built the original Dickenson-Bundy courthouse. The first court was held in the home of William Robinson at Castlewood on May 1, 1786. Justices included Alexander Barnett, Henry Smith, David Ward, Andrew Cowan, Samuel Richie, Thomas Carter, Henry Dickenson, and John Thompson. Later justices John Tate and Richard Price were added. The courthouse burned during the Revolutionary War. Henry Dickenson then constructed a two-story stone structure at a cost of $2,188.97. This structure was used as a courthouse until 1818 and is still referred to as the "Old Courthouse." When the senate proposed a 100th county, members wanted to name it "Stonewall" in honor of Gen. Stonewall Jackson. The county would have over 100 communities during its first 90 years in existence. (Photograph courtesy of the Southwest Virginia Historical and Preservation Society.)

DICKENSON COUNTY COURTHOUSE. The Dickenson County Courthouse in Clintwood was once referred to as the "wedding capital" of the area due to the large number of weddings that took place in the building. However, not all business conducted in the building is as pleasant; the area's most notorious criminals have found themselves there for trials and sentencing. (Photograph courtesy of the Southwest Virginia Historical and Preservation Society.)

HISTORIC HOLLY CREEK. Clintwood is one of three cities incorporated in Dickenson County, the other two being Clinchco and Haysi. The original name for Clintwood was Holly Creek. In 1882, the county seat was moved from Ervinton to Clintwood. This historic marker was the result of the commonwealth's program to mark historic sites for travelers. (Photograph courtesy of the Southwest Virginia Historical and Preservation Society.)

THE KILLING ROCK OF 1892. The scene at the Killing Rock is depicted in Mrs. Joan Powers Meade's work. The tragedy took place at Pound Gap on May 14, 1892. On that date, Dr. M. B. "Doc" Taylor, Calve Fleming, and Calve's brother Herman Fleming allegedly came out of the woods and began to shoot, killing Ira Mullins, his wife, Wilson Mullins, and a boy, who were making their way across the mountain in a heavily loaded wagon. John Chappel, Greenberry Harris, Jane Mullins (Wilson's wife), and John Mullins escaped. (Photograph courtesy of Dennis Reedy.)

THE CHICKEN MYSTERY SOLVED. The W. M. Ritter Lumber Company Store at McClure served the community for many years. The "chicken roost mystery" revolved around the allegation of stolen chickens, which showed up under the store. They became dinner. The only telephone in the camp was located at the store. (Photograph courtesy of Dennis Reedy).

SCAFFOLD AT WORK. Mrs. Meade's painting shows the scaffold at work in the 1890s. The painting was done from an old photograph. After the murders at Killing Rock, Doc Taylor was apprehended, tried, and convicted. He was hung for his offenses. There are four methods of hanging: the long, short, and standard drops, as well as suspension hanging. The short-drop method was used in the United States until the 19th century, when the long drop was introduced. The short drop could be a prolonged affair and was primarily for the entertainment of the public. The last public hanging was Rainey Bethea in 1936. (Photograph courtesy of Dennis Reedy.)

LICK CREEK LOGGING CAMP. The Lick Creek camp around 1927 looked much like this photograph. All camps were kept neat and clean at all times. A lobby boy swept the floors, made and changed the beds, and built and tended fires in the kitchen and lobby. In addition to the camp cars on wheels, there were also a number of portable camp houses. (Photograph courtesy of Dennis Reedy.)

RITTER COMPANY STORES. In 1925, the Ritter stores offered nine kinds of coffee, women's rayon ready-to-wear, Victrolas and Kodaks, and merchant tailors that would come in to measure for a suit. Another hot item at the store was radios. One famous brand featured was the Atwater Kent radio, which was a relatively new brand. Arthur Atwater Kent had 93 patents at his death. (Photograph courtesy of Dennis Reedy.)

THE HOTEL McCLURE. In the upper left of this photograph is the Hotel McClure around 1920. The two steam-heated sheds are where lumber that had been kiln-dried and planed was stored, especially flooring. By controlling the heat and humidity in the sheds, the lumber was kept from warping. Also visible are the planing mill, where lumber was surfaced, and the dry kiln, just beyond. (Photograph courtesy of Dennis Reedy.)

UNCLE SAM'S HOUSE. The house of "Uncle Sam" Ramsey was featured in the 1929 issue of *Hardwood Bark* magazine. The house was built entirely with Ritter lumber, with chestnut bark off the Ritter logs covering the exterior and giving it an attractive appearance. The porch ports are small tresses with the bark left on. (Photograph courtesy of Dennis Reedy.)

RAILROAD CREW AT WORK. This railroad crew works on the Calvin Fork of Lick Creek in 1933. From left to right are (first row) William Anderson (on horse), James Deel, Harvey Powers, Claude Johnson, Frank Wright, John Selfe, Albert Powers, and Sam Counts (foreman); (standing on push car) Noah Walker Counts and Arvil Counts. Sam Counts started work for Ritter as a railroad foreman in 1918. (Photograph courtesy of Dennis Reedy.)

RAIL CONSTRUCTION AT LICK CREEK. This railroad construction crew works on the Rush Branch of Lick Creek in 1923. From left to right are (seated and kneeling) Henry Duty, Alamander Silcox, ? Porter, and Sam Counts, the foreman; (standing) Carron Hay, Bill Cook, unidentified, Arvil Counts, Rual Counts, John Selfe, Holly Ray Edwards, Muncie Bostic, and Starlin Duty. The Ritter Company later moved to Frying Pan. (Photograph courtesy of Dennis Reedy.)

McClure Lumber Plant. The McClure Lumber Plant received the "E" Award during World War II, the "E" standing for excellence. The award consisted of a large flag or pennant, which was flown over the mill after the presentation of lapel pins for a job well done to staff and employees. Lumber products manufactured at McClure during World War II were used in landing and assault boats, sub chasers, mine sweepers, tugs, and PT boats, as well as Coast Guard patrol boats. Wood materials were also used in truck bodies. It was with World War II that many women found themselves going to work in the factories while husbands, brothers, fathers, and boyfriends went to fight in the war. After the war ended, the women didn't just return to the kitchens and children. Thus the introduction of women into the workforce that had been reserved for men was a direct result of World War II. (Photograph courtesy of Dennis Reedy.)

ENGINE NO. 10. Engine No. 10, pictured before the conversion from standard to narrow gauge, works as shifter at McClure around 1925. Note the large oil light on the engine. It is carrying a carload of 1-by-2¾-by-19-inch oak heading for the dry kiln, later to be worked into parquet flooring, W. M. Ritter's most famous product. The Appalachian oak flooring was manufactured at the planing mill. The small pieces of flooring known as parquet came in sizes from 9 inches to 18 inches. Parquet was laid in three distinct patterns: block, basket weave, and herringbone. Some of the smaller pieces could be glued together or fastened together with metal strips to form blocks. They were sanded, varnished, passed under lights to dry, and polished. (Photograph courtesy of Dennis Reedy.)

BEAVER CREEK RAILROAD. Foreman E. B. Dehart and his railroad crew are hard at work building a new railroad at Beaver Camp. W. M. Steele is handling the crane. Supplies such as coal, oil, and parts were hauled to the shovel on a horse-drawn sled. The logging railroad is sometimes referred to as a tram road. It was an essential part of Ritter operations. (Photograph courtesy of Dennis Reedy.)

ENGINE NO. 4. The No. 4 C/N 929 and its crew poses with a load of logs at Bear Pen Gap in 1924. Ritter owned 45 Shays. Eleven were used in Dickenson County and were maintained at the McClure Shop, which was under the supervision of "Uncle Sam" Ramsey. A fleet of 64 log cars as well as several boxcars was serviced there. (Photograph courtesy of Dennis Reedy.)

FRYING PAN TIES. Tom Ratliff, the crew boss in front, poses with his crew. From left to right are unidentified, Starlin Duty, Bill Deel, Montague Bostic, unidentified, Bryan Edwards, Henry Duty, and Basil Bostic. The railroad crew is hauling a load of oak ties near Frying Pan. The companies liked to photograph the area and its employees. (Photograph courtesy of Dennis Reedy.)

RITTER LUMBER WORKS. Ritter Lumber Company trucks loaded with large boards were a common sight. The capacity of the double mill at McClure was 80,000 feet a day. The two sections of the mill were seldom used at once, especially during the Great Depression beginning in 1929. The McClure mill averaged 42,419 feet a day for the first six months of 1928. (Photograph courtesy of Dennis Reedy.)

CLINCHCO IS BORN. These stately buildings line Main Street in Clinchco in 1920. Clinchco was built by the Clinchfield Coal Corporation in 1923. Clinchco is near the Carolina, Clinchfield, and Ohio (CC&O) Railroad and served as a mining camp. Around 1917, the Clinchfield Coal Company began mining at Clinchco, where land was bought for 10¢ to 15¢ an acre. (Photograph courtesy of Dennis Reedy.)

GULF IS BORN. As Dickenson County developed, new businesses emerged. Next to John Tipton's house, Turner Auto Sales, Inc., and the Riverside Motor Company were two of the new businesses in Riverside. Notice Turner Auto Sales endorsed and sold Gulf products. It was common for a company to identify with only one major brand in an attempt to gain consumer loyalty to them alone. (Photograph courtesy of Dennis Reedy.)

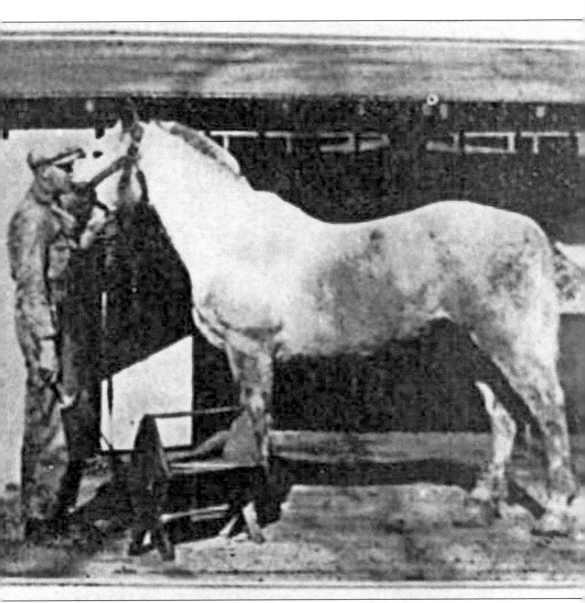

HUSKIES AT WORK. Blacksmith Frank Fletcher is pictured alongside Dutch at Lick Creek Camp around 1928. The work required of the huskies (heavy horses bred for farming and other heavy work) was often dangerous. Sometimes the logs would skid too fast, and the horses were able to dart into a clearing, releasing them from the logs, when the team driver called out "Jay-hole!" That meant the logs could continue to proceed down the hill while the horse was away from the danger. Companies regarded the animals as more valuable than the employees. The blacksmith who shod horses was a farrier. A blacksmith could usually double as a blade smith and locksmith. He could do repairs to logging chains and axe heads. (Photograph courtesy of Dennis Reedy.)

SECRET TO SUCCESS. Grady Baker is pictured with his sidekick, Peanut. Baker had an interesting philosophy about success; he was often quoted by friends as saying, "In order to be a success in life, never make the same mistake twice"—quite an interesting statement for a hardworking man that took a simplistic approach to the age-old question. (Photograph courtesy of Dennis Reedy.)

DICK AND CLYDE. Teamster Ralph Keller poses with Dick (left) and Clyde in 1921. The horses were said to be the best that money could buy. The men who drove the teams were known as team drivers or teamsters. A team could pull several logs at a time depending on the size of the logs and the terrain. (Photograph courtesy of Dennis Reedy.)

W. M. RITTER. W. M. Ritter, the founder and president of the W. M. Ritter Lumber Company, is seen here around 1940. Ritter, the youngest of 10 children, was the son of Franklin and Elizabeth Morris Ritter, who was a member of the Morris family that produced Robert Morris of Philadelphia, the Revolutionary patriot who largely financed the colonies in their struggle against the mother country. (Photograph courtesy of Dennis Reedy.)

RITTER'S FIRST OFFICE. This was the W. M. Ritter Lumber Company's first office at Welsh, West Virginia, used from 1896 until 1899. In 1899, the offices were moved to Columbus, Ohio. In 1903, the general office was moved from the Schultz Building to the Harrison Building, later called the Huntington Bank Building. In 1915, the general office was moved to the Peruna Building. (Photograph courtesy of Dennis Reedy.)

DOUBLE BAND MILL. The W. M. Ritter Lumber Company's mill at McClure in the 1920s had a daily capacity of 80,000 board feet. The building with the three tall stacks was the boiler room. In front of the boiler room was the water tank for the Shay engines. The physical plant and accompanying structures at McClure were similar to those at Fremont but on a larger scale. A planing mill and dry kiln serving both operations were built at McClure during 1918–1919. (Photograph courtesy of Dennis Reedy.)

WORKER SALARY BASE. The men were paid different wages from 10¢ to 15¢ an hour according to the jobs they performed. The men had to pay 60¢ a day for food and lodging at the boardinghouse. If they rented company housing, the rent was deducted from their paychecks. There were other deductions such as electric and medical bills. Advances on paychecks would also be deducted. If they bought items in advance at the company store, those deductions would also be withheld. Many times, the workers received no pay or owed money on payday. (Photograph courtesy of Dennis Reedy.)

Two

FOUNDERS AND BUILDERS

McClure Bottom around 1920. Notice the machine shop in the lower left. Six of the company's Shay engines can be seen on the yard above the shop. Sand was scooped from the river and dried in the small building near the engines for use on the locomotives to keep the wheels from slipping on a steep grade or wet rail. The place that later became known as McClure was selected by the Virginia General Assembly in 1880 as the governmental seat for the newly formed county. Citizens in the western part of the county were not satisfied with the chosen site and struggled to have it relocated. While the dispute was being settled, the county seat was located at Nora, about three miles south. A map of the area showed only McClure River, not McClure the town. Legend says the stream and the town were named for an explorer who was killed by Native Americans. (Photograph courtesy of Dennis Reedy.)

FRYING PAN CAMP. Camp cars are pictured on Frying Pan Creek. The cars were the solution to the problem of transportation to logging camps. The store (or commissary) and office were usually combined on the end of the string of cars. The camp stores were well stocked. On each end of the lobby were the sleeping areas—railroad cars accommodating 16 to 20 men each. (Photograph courtesy of Dennis Reedy.)

THE FOUNDER AND HEIR. Jim Damron (left) assists W. M. Ritter as the great lumber baron makes his last trip to the Red Jacket mine in September 1947. Jim Damron started with the Ritter Lumber Company as a laborer at the planing mill at McClure. Damron, a native of Clintwood, operated a taxi before going to work for Ritter. He would drive Ritter around the area when he visited the county. (Photograph courtesy of Dennis Reedy.)

WORK ON CANEY CREEK. Russell Stevens (left) and John Shortridge pose with their team. The road is called a pole road, over which the logs were dragged on Caney Creek around 1940. Usually logs were dragged over the ground. A crew of men called road swamps cut brush for the roads, while men known as road monkeys used picks and shovels to do the grade work. (Photograph courtesy of Dennis Reedy.)

TRAMMEL COMPANY STORE. Seen here is the company store and post office at Trammel, Virginia. The company built, owned, operated, and controlled the housing, hospitals, schools, local governments, and company stores, and it provided free land to build churches. The company store was the only place a worker and his family could use the company-issued scrip. (Photograph courtesy of Dennis Reedy.)

BIG BRANCH CAMP. The Big Branch camp in 1923 was located around Clintwood on the waters of the Cranes Nest and Pound Rivers and tributary streams. Some of the campsites in 1926 were at the mouth of Tarpon Branch on the headwaters of Cane Creek and Mill Creek 3,300 feet up the side of the Cumberland Mountains. Homes usually were of no more than one style of design, with a block of single dwellings and a block of duplexes. Company houses ran from single-dwelling duplexes, usually side by side, to boardinghouses for single men. Houses for the bosses were usually built of better materials. Rent was automatically deducted from employees' paychecks for the use of the company housing and electricity. (Photograph courtesy of Dennis Reedy.)

LICK CREEK CAMP CARS. Note the bunk beds with the white bed linens visible through the door in these camp cars on Lick Creek. On each end of the lobby were the sleeping areas. The railroad cars could accommodate 16 to 20 men in each car. This is where the single workers or those that boarded away from home would stay. (Photograph courtesy of Dennis Reedy.)

JIM DAMRON AROUND 1940. James W. "Jim" Damron was president of the W. M. Ritter Lumber Company. Jim Damron of Clintwood, Virginia, was the third president of the Ritter organization, with W. M. Pryor serving as chairman from 1935 to 1945. Later Damron would serve as chairman of the board while "Little William" Ritter was president. (Photograph courtesy of Dennis Reedy.)

HAMER LUMBER COMPANY. The J. P. Hamer Lumber Company was the only band mill remaining in Southwest Virginia by the end of the boom days. It was located between Norton and Appalachia. The mill operations had been sophisticated, with Ritter becoming famous for his parquet flooring. (Photograph courtesy of Dennis Reedy.)

RITTER'S MASSIVE OPERATIONS. The planing mill in Lower Elk is an example of how large the W. M. Ritter Lumber Company operations were. This facility had everything to manage the wood from start to finish, from the dry kilns to the loading shed to the engine room and ice plant. This also included the warehouse and steam-heated hardwood flooring areas. (Photograph courtesy of Dennis Reedy.)

FRYING PAN WORK CREW. These men are waiting to be hauled up the hill to their work site in 1927. Families lived in the wood camps rent free and were also provided free coal to burn in their cook stove. There was no electricity in the camps, kerosene lamps being used exclusively. No running water existed in the camps. As it was so difficult to get men and teams back and forth to the job sites, the temporary camps were created. These portable camps consisted of 8 to 12 railroad cars housing the camp store, boardinghouse, and lobby. The camp stores were well stocked for their limited size. If the customer wanted merchandise that was not available in the camp, a store order could be sent to the main store at Fremont or McClure. (Photograph courtesy of Dennis Reedy.)

TYPICAL MOUNTAIN COUPLE. Alexander and Melvina Hill were a typical mountain couple of the day. He was born in 1849 and lived until 1927. He and Melvina were married in 1873. It was virtually unheard of for couples in the area to divorce. It was common for the man to marry again if his wife died. (Photograph courtesy of Dennis Reedy.)

PLANE CRASH MARKER. This grave marker is for Paul Bennett, Dale Coleman, and Jack Stockdale, who were killed in a plane crash on August 25, 1965. The location is known locally as Airplane Crash Rock. It is located at Birch Knob, Virginia, six miles north of Clintwood in the Jefferson National Forest. (Photograph courtesy of Dennis Reedy.)

LARGE MOUNTAIN FAMILY. The family of John Henry "Long John" and Emma (Stanley) Yates poses about 1920. It was typical for families to include 10 or more children. Usually two to three were lost in the early years to various causes of death, but it was common for parents to raise to adulthood as many as 10 to 15 children. (Photograph courtesy of Dennis Reedy.)

COUNTY JAIL LOGS. The lower story of this building contains the logs from the first Dickenson County jail in Clintwood. Justice in the mountains in the early years was very different. Many times, the citizens themselves took the matter into their own hands and dispensed justice with the Bible as the law. (Photograph courtesy of Dennis Reedy.)

Poppy John and Gulf. John "Pop" Molinary stands in front of the Gulf service station. The Gulf Oil Corporation or GOC was a major oil company from the beginning of the century to the 1980s. The business that became Gulf Oil Corporation started in 1901 with the discovery of oil in Spindletop, Texas. Gulf introduced significant commercial and technical innovations into the business, including the first drive-in service station in 1911 that also offered free air to motorists and complimentary road maps. By 1941, Gulf was the eighth-largest corporation in the world and number nine in 1979. Gulf was one of the so-called Seven Sisters of oil magnets, but by the mid-1970s, the industry began to change. In 1984, the Gulf Oil Corporation ceased being an independent company when it merged with Standard Oil of California, better known as Chevron. (Photograph courtesy of Dennis Reedy.)

SANDY RIDGE TUNNEL. W. C. Hattan inspects the north portal of the Sandy Ridge Tunnel in Trammel, Virginia, around 1912. It was a long and tedious process to cut through the mountainside to build the necessary tunnels to accommodate the trains that needed to haul the coal. The tunnels opened up the area for new industry to arrive. (Photograph courtesy of Dennis Reedy.)

BOY SCOUTS OF AMERICA. Troop 42 of McClure was organized in 1951. The national Boy Scouts organization was started in 1907 by Robert Baden Powell, a lieutenant general of the British army. These scouts constructed their own boats from small wooden runners converted with canvas. Each boat cost $100 to construct. (Photograph courtesy of Dennis Reedy.)

MEAL TIME IN CAMP. These men are timber cutters at dinnertime near Lick Creek Camp, Virginia. The hours were long, but the food was plentiful. The logging companies had at least two cooks on duty at all times to prepare the meals and do the cleanup for the loggers. (Photograph courtesy of Dennis Reedy.)

THE PROPER SAW DEMONSTRATIONS. Here is W. M. Kennedy of Maben Woods demonstrating how not to carry the saw and how to carry it. (Photograph courtesy of Dennis Reedy.)

MOUNTAIN COUPLES TRANSPORTATION. These couples could be on a Sunday afternoon outing or going to visit family or friends. Transportation was primitive in the Cumberland Mountains until the logging industry started building roads to get to the timber the mountains held. Many old Native American paths were the only roads used up until that time, which meant that couples only traveled when it was absolutely necessary to take care of business such as legal matters or to pay taxes. Another major reason was for funerals or weddings. Possibly these dressed-up couples were on their way to a wedding, as they look very happy to be out on such a beautiful day with their husbands or boyfriends—probably husbands since no chaperone is evident in this photograph. Chaperones were necessary for any proper couple during their courting period before the marriage. (Photograph courtesy of Dennis Reedy.)

SOUTH SANDY RIDGE. This photograph depicts the south approach to the Sandy Ridge Tunnel showing the dump trestle and train in Dante, Virginia, in August 1914. The tunnel saved the company a great deal of money in expenses in getting the coal to market on time. That enabled them to sign contracts with larger corporations, which made the area boom for a while. (Photograph courtesy of Dennis Reedy.)

SANDY CONCRETE CAR. With the logging and mining industries bringing a boom to the county for an extended period of years, they started building. Many of the buildings that were built in the 1920s and 1930s of concrete are still standing today as a testament to the craftsmanship of those builders. (Photograph courtesy of Dennis Reedy.)

CAMP HOUSING BOOM. Sara Hatton inspects her new home at Squirrel Camp around 1912. The company housing system was quite advanced for its time. All the houses were built in a row, and there were usually one or two designs. The houses were usually painted in a distinct color such as green or white. They can still be recognized in the older parts of these communities today. The houses were usually one or two bedrooms. The renters or employees paid the company a rental fee each month for use of the house. If an employee was fired or quit, they had to pack up and leave immediately. The bosses had houses at the other end of the community. The houses were larger with a few more amenities, which were appropriate for their titles within the company. The company store, hotel, hospital, school, and church were all within that small community. (Photograph courtesy of Dennis Reedy.)

TOMS CREEK COMPANY STORE. Shown here is the large company store at Toms Creek. The company stores were vital to the community. The stores were well stocked, and delivery was free if a costumer requested it. The stores also were of service in that the loggers and later miners could buy on credit that would be deducted from their paychecks. (Photograph courtesy of Dennis Reedy.)

CLINCHCO V. CLINTWOOD. The Frying Pan and Clinchco or possibly Clintwood baseball teams take a rest. The C on the uniforms stood for both Clintwood and Clinchco. On Saturdays, the companies provided transportation to the games. The games were taken so serious that some companies recruited college players to play on their team. (Photograph courtesy of Dennis Reedy.)

FREELING POST OFFICE. This is all that remains of the old Freeling Post Office. The mail was originally transported from Raven, Virginia, on horseback to the area. Then the company stores started handling it. As progress arrived and the system became more sophisticated, the government started building post offices. One like this is rare to even see today. (Photograph courtesy of Dennis Reedy.)

WINTERS AT RIVERSIDE. In this picture of Riverside around 1954, the grocery store is on the right along with the Clinchco Café and Coney's service station in the distance. Winters in the mountains are notorious for shutting everything and everyone down for weeks. It is common to have snows of a foot or more. (Photograph courtesy of Dennis Reedy.)

W. M. PRYOR. W. M. Pryor served as chairman and former president of the W. M. Ritter Lumber Company in 1940. The company that started with a $1,500 loan had by 1924 grown so much that its founder, W. M. Ritter, had been called to serve as an executive member of the Council of National Defense, with the start of the United States' participation in World War I. At the end of 1924, Ritter startled the nation when he gave away $3 million worth of stock to employees of his company, who deserved it by being loyal. Pres. Calvin Coolidge was so impressed that he called Ritter to the White House to discuss it and followed it with a complimentary letter in which he praised this act as a fine step towards happier employer-employee relations. This action also brought up the first test of the newly passed gift tax feature of the Revenue Act. (Photograph courtesy of Dennis Reedy.)

PRIMITIVE PASTOR LIPPS. The first organized church in Darwin was known as the Lost Meeting House. It was at the mouth of Honey Camp. It was the old Primitive Baptist, with Morgan Lipps as its pastor. Visiting ministers were James Smith, D. H. Riner, Billy Hale, and George Buchanan. (Photograph courtesy of Dennis Reedy.)

CHILDREN IN CAMPS. Notice the load of timber on the railroad car in the background of this photograph. The child is obviously fascinated by the camera, as photography was new in the area in the early 1920s. Children in the camps always had plenty of other children to play with, as they all lived next door to each other. (Photograph courtesy of Dennis Reedy.)

KOPP'S OFFICE AT FREMONT. The building across the tracks served as A. A. Kopp's office and later as the Fremont Post Office. These children had much to occupy them. They did not have the high-tech toys of today, but they did invent their own games such as fox and geese, kickball, and swimming in the creeks. Motion pictures were becoming popular in the 1920s, and the community buildings also doubled as movie houses. Dance clubs were formed, and the company trains carried the employees to different locations to perform and entertain the families. A hand-packed dirt tennis court was located on Caney Creek. A croquet ground was also on Caney, as was the baseball diamond. Gospel singing and basketball also helped to entertain the men and their families during their free time. The baseball games were well attended. In 1927, *Hardwood Bark* magazine stated that Lower Elk fans received a sad surprise when the "Caney Nine" defeated their invincible warriors. (Photograph courtesy of Dennis Reedy.)

Three

SCHOOLS

EARLY SCHOOL BUSES. The old Ervinton High School in Nora, Virginia, is pictured about 1936 showing two early buses. The one on the left is a Chevrolet, while the one on the right is a Ford. Both of them are about 1934 models. The men are, from left to right, Roosevelt Kiser, Buddy Stanley (the school custodian), and Everette Bise, who drove the bus for Rube Wright. Buses at that time were privately owned instead of county property. Wayne Works is widely credited with creating what became school buses. In 1886, he was making horse-drawn school carriages many people called "kid hacks" (hack is a term for certain types of horse-drawn carriages). By 1914, he had dropped a wooden kid onto an automobile chassis, and the school bus was born. But it is Dr. Frank Cyr who is the father of the yellow school bus. The color was selected so black lettering could be seen in darkness. (Photograph courtesy of Dennis Reedy.)

OLD BISE SCHOOL. The first room of this two-room building was constructed in 1915. A second room was added in 1923 by contractors Kennedy and Dotson at a cost of $2,000. This school was discontinued at the end of the 1963–1964 session. The first school was taught in an old building used for a church and Odd Fellows hall. (Photograph courtesy of Dennis Reedy.)

AN UNKNOWN OLD SCHOOL. This photograph depicts a two-room school under construction at an undetermined location within the county in the 1920s. Included in the picture are George Burchette (left), L. A. Priode, M. E. Senter, and T. Washom Bise. (Photograph courtesy of Dennis Reedy.)

THE CLINCHCO TEACHERS. These ladies of Clinchco may have been teachers. The building in the center behind them was the school at that time but was formerly the first company store built in Clinchco about 1916. A portion of the 10 seven-room apartments, one of which housed the teachers and was called the Teachers Cottage, is visible to the right. (Photograph courtesy of Dennis Reedy.)

CLINTWOOD PUBLIC SCHOOL. The Clintwood Public School and Normal College was erected in 1904. Prof. Milton W. Remines served as principal. From 1909 until 1922, the building housed the Clintwood High School and Clintwood Elementary School. The site is now occupied by the school board office. During the Civil War, the Clintwood School was used for only three months in 1865. (Photograph courtesy of Dennis Reedy.)

SUPERINTENDENT OF SCHOOLS. Willie A. Dyer served as superintendent of the county schools from 1905 until 1909. Dyer was also a schoolteacher for 13 years in the county school system. In 1901–1902, he taught at Cold Spring School and received a salary of $30 per month. The first year he taught, he received only $24 per month. In 1903, Dyer taught at Trammel. In 1904, he bought out the French Mercantile Company and sold goods at the Forks of McClure for an extended period of time. In 1905, he was appointed division superintendent of schools for the county at a salary of $20 per month. Dyer made it a point to visit all the schools within his jurisdiction. His duties included attending board meetings, issuing certificates, holding exams, and visiting schools. (Photograph courtesy of Dennis Reedy.)

Big Oak School. The tall gentleman behind the children is teacher Roley Stanley in 1913 with his class. Pictured are, from left to right, as follows: (first row) Virgie Owens, Eva Stanley, Bertha Owens, Virgie Stanley, unidentified, Grace Stanley, Verta Stanley, Julia Reedy, Bill Fields, Kemper Fields, Alice Fields, and ? Fields; (second row) Elise Fleming, Emma Stanley, Lula Kennedy, Willie Stanley, Leon Fields, Willard Stanley, Stewart Childress, Hattie Stanley, and Lydia Childress. It was very difficult for children to go to school in the early 20th century. The first schools were generally subscription schools. The teacher was paid a certain amount per student enrolled in the class. When farm work or chores at home demanded, the children were kept out of school to help with the work while their fathers worked in the mines or logging camps—it was a necessity to survive. Students often had to walk three or more miles to get to school in various weather conditions. (Photograph courtesy of Dennis Reedy.)

CLINCHCO TEACHERS AROUND 1941. The Clinchco teachers for the academic year 1941–1942 are, from left to right, (first row) Louise Sutherland, Glady Rudder, Dorsey Reedy, Samantha Remines, Val Hilton, Hazel C. Parker, and Janice McCoy; (second row) principal Clyde Reedy, Major Arwood, Claude Carty, and assistant principal Edgar Alley. The starting salary for teachers was $24 per month. (Photograph courtesy of Dennis Reedy.)

OLD ABNER GAP. The first Abner Gap School was a one-room building constructed of logs and mud, but later a more modern structure of planks was built. The small school fit the needs of the community when it was first settled in 1860, when wealthy landowner Samuel Endicutt and his family built in the area. (Photograph courtesy of Dennis Reedy.)

BUS RIDE AT FREMONT. Area Fremont children wait for the school bus around 1954. By 1954, children could ride a bus versus walking several miles to school like earlier generations. By the early 1950s, more parents saw the importance of sending their children to school. They willingly made the sacrifices necessary to give their children an education. (Photograph courtesy of Dennis Reedy.)

CLINTWOOD'S GREENWOOD SCHOOL. The two-room Greenwood School was built by D. G. Kelly of Clintwood in 1911 for a little over $800. In 1925, W. O. Deel was contracted to add two additional rooms at a cost of $2,800. One room was used for a cafeteria and three rooms for classrooms in later years. The school closed at the conclusion of the 1968–1969 academic year. (Photograph courtesy of Dennis Reedy.)

NORA'S LITTLE SCHOOL. The two-room Nora School was built by McCorkle Lumber Company in 1917 and used until the Ervinton School was ready for occupancy in 1936. The present-day Ervinton High School on Open Fork opened in 1955. Nora had no school until Mrs. H. F. Binns began to teach in the church. The number of pupils was irregular due to camp families moving in and out. In 1924, the lumber company moved away, so the school remained small. Nora's first name was Open Fork. Later it was called Ervinton. When the Rasnakes had the post office, they called the area Stratton. It was the county seat until Capt. John P. Chase was elected to the legislature, at which time he had the county seat moved to his home, then Holly Creek, now Clintwood. The next postmaster was Jack Dorton. Dorton named the area Nora after his wife. (Photograph courtesy of Dennis Reedy.)

THE WAKENVA SCHOOL. The Wakenva School was built in 1938 with Works Progress Administration (WPA) funds at a cost of $3,356.19. The first year of operation, Jack Hilton, who transferred from Roaring Fork, taught five months. The school had two teachers each of the next two years. The fourth year, only one teacher was at the school. The school closed at the end of the 1964–1965 academic year. (Photograph courtesy of Dennis Reedy.)

STEINMAN'S LITTLE SCHOOL. The Steinman School is seen as it looked in 1954. The school had been abandoned by this time. The name Steinman originated from the company mining coal in the neighborhood, Steinman Coal Corporation. The company began operations in 1918. The school was located on the west bank of the McClure Creek in the Willis District. (Photograph courtesy of Dennis Reedy.)

TRACE FORKS SCHOOL. The Trace Fork School was sometimes called Lyons Fork School. As there were no school buildings in the beginning, most classes were taught in old dwelling houses, churches, or stores. Trace Fork was built in 1921. It started out with only two rooms. In 1938, a third room was added. This was a joint venture with Wise County, each owning half. (Photograph courtesy of Dennis Reedy.)

BIG TOMS SCHOOL. As the Toms Creek School shows, not all county schools were simple one- or two-room structures. Coal mining started in Toms Bottom in 1917. It was located in the Breaks of the Cumberland Mountains on the CC&O Railroad line, near the Kentucky line. The Bartlick Smokeless coal mines operated close by. (Photograph courtesy of Dennis Reedy.)

STEINMAN AROUND 1950. Steinman is seen as it appeared in the 1950s. The school is the last building on the hill near the left center of this photograph. The Steinman Development Company and other companies had extensive holdings in the area. The holdings were put into the Wakenva Coal Company with C. Bascom Slemp and S. R. Jennings as officers. (Photograph courtesy of Dennis Reedy.)

THE STONEWALL SCHOOL. The Stonewall School was built in 1926 on property deeded by Nathaniel and Polly Rose to the county. Henry Ratliff served as the contractor. The Stonewall community was densely settled. The school was named after one of the citizens and ran for nine months out of the year. This was the first school to run for nine months in that area. (Photograph courtesy of Dennis Reedy.)

An Academic Giant. Prof. Milton Remines was a dominating figure in the academic world of Dickenson County. He served as superintendent of schools for a number of years. He had the difficult task of bringing education to a rural area that had to worry about surviving from day to day. Enthusiasm was great when Professor Remines arrived at the Hale lot near W. M. Merrick's home in 1898. He was assisted by Hattie Phipps, Alice Robinson, and James Altizer. However, around March 1902, the structure burned and the term was finished at the Methodist church. Soon a new building was erected, and the influence of Professor Remines was evident. An act was passed by the Virginia General Assembly on March 9, 1903, authorizing issuance of $3,000 to $7,000 in bonds by the Clintwood school district trustees for 25 years to complete a new building. It would be one of the most outstanding buildings in the state at that time. It was called the Clintwood Normal College. (Photograph courtesy of Dennis Reedy.)

THE OLD CANE SCHOOL. The Cane Creek School was a one-room structure built in 1913. The first Native Americans known in the county came from Russell County about the year 1850 to Cane. They captured a white girl and spent that first night on Cane Creek. The school was used for about 10 years and ran three months a year. (Photograph courtesy of Dennis Reedy.)

NEW ABNER GAP. The school was built in 1938 with the aid of the WPA at a cost of $16,000. The New Abner Gap School was unusual in that it was the only brick two-room building constructed in the county at that time. It also contained an office and conference room. (Photograph courtesy of Dennis Reedy.)

KENNEDY CONSTRUCTION COMPANY. The Middle Branch School was built in 1922 by B. F. Kennedy. It was difficult to provide supplies for the first schools. The woodpile often served for seats and one's knees for desks. The elementary spelling book was one of the few books used. Students practiced spelling aloud. (Photograph courtesy of Dennis Reedy.)

THE POOR MAN'S STORE. The exact time of the Prater settlement is unknown, but the school was built in 1935 and closed in 1969. It was sold the same year and became "The Poor Man's Store." Money was scarce, and even after a few small stores were built, the people bought the few things they needed with produce and ginseng. (Photograph courtesy of Dennis Reedy.)

THE BEAR PEN. The Bear Pen School received its name due to a bear trap. Bear Pen lies in the Cumberland Mountains. Elbert M. Fulton, later a prominent Wise County lawyer, taught there. The log building on Pound River above the mouth of Bear Pen Creek was used for religious worship as well as school purposes. Monthly meetings were conducted there for perhaps 50 years, but it later became private property and was torn down. The Bear Pen community had few settlers and in that way was similar to another former settlement, Goldsmith's deserted village. Some of the bottoms along the river have been cleared up and cultivated. While workmen were repairing the public roads, they ran across a huge cliff below the mouth of Bear Pen Creek. They found human bones embedded under the large flat rock. (Photograph courtesy of Dennis Reedy.)

WEST DANTE SCHOOL. The West Dante School was built in 1917 by B. F. Kennedy with new additions added in 1926. In the beginning, only three families lived in and around Dante. The population would grow with the emergence of mining. West Dante was first called Turkey Foot. The reason for that is the shape of the creek marker. The citizens built the school. (Photograph courtesy of Dennis Reedy.)

OLD FLINT SCHOOL. The Old Flint School is located on the lower end of Sandy Ridge. Unlike many area schools, the Old Flint School was built totally by the citizens. Citizens who could not help work on the house donated their part in money or supplies. The walls of this school are at least 10 inches thick. (Photograph courtesy of Dennis Reedy.)

BEAR PEN GRADUATES. Pictured is the graduating class of Bear Pen School for the academic year 1948–1949. The Bear Pen School was a consolidation of three schools: Brush Creek, Fairview, and Kilgore. It was established in 1918. There have been seven schools, the first six averaging five-month terms. The seventh established the nine-month school year. (Photograph courtesy of Dennis Reedy.)

OPEN FORK SCHOOL. This two-room structure was built in 1917. The date the school closed is not available, but the building was sold in October 1969, so the closing date was probably close to that. The original structure was built in 1885. The house was made of logs lapped together at each end and daubed with mud and moss, with windows two feet wide on each side. (Photograph courtesy of Dennis Reedy.)

TRACE FORK PAINTING. The old Trace Fork School is being painted around 1938. The first school was taught near Jarvey Robinson's home in an old log dwelling house by Henderson Dean. Trace Fork is sometimes referred to as Lyons Fork. The school was built in 1921. (Photograph courtesy of Dennis Reedy.)

KENNEDY AND DOTSON BUILDERS. The Viers School was built by Kennedy and Dotson in 1917 at a cost of $2,500. It was abandoned long before this photograph was taken in 1954. The first rough log schoolhouse was built on Laurel Branch in 1878. It had a fireplace about six feet wide and only two windows. (Photograph courtesy of Dennis Reedy.)

EARLY SCHOOL IN BARTLICK. The first room of this school was built in 1912. The second room was added in 1916. The school remained in operation until 1961. The first schools in Bartlick were taught in the homes that were available. The old Harve Colley house was once used as a schoolhouse. In the early 1890s, the first school was built. It was on the Harve Colley property. It was a small structure with dirt floors with a fireplace at one end. It was condemned by the school board after about five years because of its smallness. The county was in a financial crisis, and no money was available for a new school. The Turner School was used during that period of time. In 1899, Crockett Owens was paid $40 to put up the walls of a new school. Once the logs were on the site, they had a house-raising party, and a new school emerged. (Photograph courtesy of Dennis Reedy.)

THE OLD WAKENVA SCHOOL. The Old Wakenva School stands no more. Like many of the schools, churches, and buildings that started the county, the history gets lost. As generations die, they take with them the history of that area. Much of the history that exists owes that fact to superintendent of schools Joshua Hoge Taylor Sutherland when he had his teachers keep reports. (Photograph courtesy of Dennis Reedy.)

MOUNT CARMEL LEGACY. The Mount Carmel School around 1938 shows students waiting on the teacher. The school was discontinued before 1954, and little is known of its existence. The students that attended these small schools usually attended school once the farming, canning, and other household chores were completed. (Photograph courtesy of Dennis Reedy.)

THE ENDLESS STRUGGLE. The Cranes Nest School was built in 1950. The need for the school was great, as students had to be sent to the Bise, Kerr, or Dickenson Memorial High School in Clintwood. The community took a while to decide on the location because they were divided into two separate factions. Petitions went before the school board, which decided the school would be located near the Cranes Nest River by the state highway between Clintwood and Fremont. Once built, the school enjoyed a high attendance, averaging about 48 students a year. The school faced endless struggles to get equipment; at one point, only one blackboard existed for the entire school. Some of the early teachers included Mrs. Thomas M. Flannagan and Virgil Skeen. The first settler in Cranes Nest was Weddington Vanover, who built the first log house. (Photograph courtesy of Dennis Reedy.)

The Class of 1938. The Dickenson Memorial High School class of 1938 is pictured on graduation day. The ancient custom of wearing gowns and caps goes back to Europe in the 11th and 12th centuries and later at Oxford and Cambridge Universities. It was recognized that the caps and gowns gave such functions more character and were more impressive, which increased attendance at the commencement functions. (Photograph courtesy of Dennis Reedy.)

The Kenady School. The Walter Kenady School was built in 1913. It is one of three that are no longer existing, the others being the Pine Grove School near Lyons Post Office and Zion Hill. The patrons built the school. The seats were made of split poles. Holes were bored in the round side of the poles, and legs were driven into them. (Photograph courtesy of Dennis Reedy.)

THE ERVINGTON REBELS. The Ervington High School is still being used to help educate the county's young. The mascot painted on a wall is a rebel. The schools take the business of mascots seriously, putting the image on everything from class rings to the yearbook and letterman jackets. (Photograph courtesy of Southwest Virginia Historical and Preservation Society.)

DICKENSON COUNTY HIGH SCHOOL. The Dickenson County Memorial and Industrial High School serves the Clintwood area as a multi-purpose building, serving the county's academic and industrial needs at the same time. The building is used as a landmark to find one's way in the town. (Photograph courtesy of Southwest Virginia Historical and Preservation Society.)

MᴄCʟᴜʀᴇ's Cᴏᴍᴍᴜɴɪᴛʏ Sᴄʜᴏᴏʟ Bᴜɪʟᴅɪɴɢ ᴀʀᴏᴜɴᴅ 1929. The functions of community buildings in logging and mining camps were two-fold. They provided a place for a meeting, whether for the Bridge Club or for workers being instructed in the proper way to perform their jobs. A poolroom and barbershop could also be found in such buildings, as well as church and Sunday school services. The McClure community building doubled as a school. Buildings were also used for dances or socials featuring top-notch bands such as the Ohio Melody Boys, a six-piece orchestra from Ironton, Ohio, that played at the opening dance for the building on December 8, 1922. The company ran a special train from Clinchco through Fremont picking up people for the dance. There were dance clubs at both Fremont and McClure. The community building was the center of life in the mining and logging towns. (Photograph courtesy of Dennis Reedy.)

Four

CHURCHES

THE COUNTY'S LEGACY. The Bible school class poses in front of the Old Wakenva School around 1928. The school and church were the cornerstones of community life. The early revival services were held in peoples' homes. The minister stayed with the family for a few days before going on to the next town. It gave the community a chance to get outside information when it usually took weeks for news to travel from community to community and the mail took longer. People took their religious beliefs seriously, showing respect for God, family, and country. The religious groups included the Baptists and Methodists, with communities generally having at least one Catholic church. The companies that controlled the economy in the county viewed the churches in the same manner, providing the land and materials to build many of them. (Photograph courtesy of Dennis Reedy.)

ONCE A BOARDINGHOUSE. The McClure Methodist Church, pictured around 1949, was formerly a boardinghouse, or clubhouse. It was built by the W. M. Ritter Lumber Company and was called Hotel Ritter. Ritter's American log loader, in the foreground, used to cut trees and brush, was for years run by Patton Moore. (Photograph courtesy of Dennis Reedy.)

DEACONESS BINNS AND CHILDREN. Deaconess ? Binns stands with a group of children in front of the Old St. Stephens Church in Nora about 1930. The first preaching in the county was at the mouth of Hatchet. Sunday school at St. Stephens was held every Sunday with Thursday night services. A preacher would arrive every other Thursday. The deaconess handled the services otherwise. (Photograph courtesy of Dennis Reedy.)

Barbara's Sunday Class.
Barbara Parks poses with her
Sunday school class about 1953.
By the 1950s, the roads were
more accessible, making church
attendance easier for the residents.
Before that, despite bad conditions,
people would walk many miles
to attend church once a month,
visiting with family and friends
after the service. (Photograph
courtesy of Dennis Reedy.)

Missionary at Ritter. Fannie
Diffenduffer was a missionary in
Ritter's lumber camp at Stratton,
Virginia, about 1935. Ritter Lumber
provided academic and religious
opportunities and instruction for
its employees. The Frying Pan
camp was moved to Stratton
on the waters of the McClure
River in 1935. While moving
the camp from Russell Fork, to
Stratton, the store car went into
the river. (Photograph courtesy of
Dennis Reedy.)

LITTLE RACHEL CHAPEL. The little Rachel Chapel was established in 1936. Before that, it served as a school for children that had attended the Kenady School, about one and a half miles from the chapel on the main road to Coeburn. The first teacher was Belle Dotson, a local girl. Hampton Osborne from Lee County served as teacher from 1928 to 1929. The Freewill Baptist Church served as school and church. Church names and locations varied throughout the community. Sumac Grove got its name from sumacs that grew nearby, and the denomination was Primitive Baptist. The Baptists were divided into two groups: the Primitive Baptist (hardshells) and the regular Baptists (softshells). The difference between the two groups is in the belief of the meaning of the resurrection. Many members of the church would give out invitations to other members to go home with them and enjoy the food prepared as only mountain homemakers could. It was known as the "Sunday-go-to-meetin' dinner." (Photograph courtesy of Dennis Reedy.)

CLINTWOOD'S STAINED GLASS. The Clintwood United Methodist Church has sandstone walls and stained-glass windows. It is those windows that make the church famous throughout the community. The sandstone makes the church one of the true treasures down the street from the courthouse. The church is one of the few in the area that is built of sandstone and not wood or brick. (Photograph courtesy of Dennis Reedy.)

CLINCHCO MISSIONARY BAPTISTS. The Clinchco Missionary Baptist Church in Clinchco is one of many local churches for the county. John Smyth in 1610 founded the first Baptist church in Holland with 36 charter members. They believe that baptism is for believers only. (Photograph courtesy of Southwest Virginia Historical and Preservation Society.)

CLINTWOOD AND THE BAPTISTS. It is incorrect to apply the term church to any Baptist segment except the local church. The largest of the 20 or more Baptist groups is the Southern Baptist Convention, with over 12 million members. The largest Northern segment is the American Baptist church with 1.5 million members. When being introduced to a Baptist clergyman, is proper to call him minister. They are only addressed as pastor if they lead the congregation. The Free Will Baptist denomination can trace its origins back to 1727, when Paul Palmer organized a church at Chowan, North Carolina. The northern segment, or the Randall movement as it is commonly referred to, started with Benjamin Randall's congregation in New Hampshire. Both groups believe in the twin doctrines of free will and free salvation. In 1935, the two groups of Free Will Baptists came together under the title of the Cooperative General Association. (Photograph courtesy of the Southwest Virginia Historical and Preservation Society.)

ST. JOSEPH'S CATHOLICS. St. Joseph's in Clintwood is one of the county's few Catholic churches. St. Joseph is the husband of Mary and father of Jesus of Nazareth. He is the patron saint of workers and was declared the patron saint and protector of the Universal Catholic Church by Pope Pius IX in 1870. (Photograph courtesy of the Southwest Virginia Historical and Preservation Society.)

THE CHURCH OF CHRIST. The United Church of Christ was born out of a combination of four groups. The Congregational churches of the English Reformation with Puritan New England roots and the Christian Church of frontier days were its beginning. The other two denominations were the Evangelical Synod and the Reformed Church. They all share the commitment to religious expression. (Photograph courtesy of Southwest Virginia Historical and Preservation Society.)

THE VALLEY BAPTISTS. The Valley View Freewill Baptist Church was founded on July 14, 1914, in the Yates Gap section of the county. The early records of the church are scarce but indicate they met under an apple tree on the property adjacent to the present church. Later a church building was erected on land donated by Bishop Yates. The name Valley View was chosen by Willie Stallard. They adopted the Baptist Faith and Message, which serves as a guide to understanding their beliefs. The Baptists also have a group called the Independent Fundamental Baptists, who are independent of the Baptist convention or other associations and are more conservative in their beliefs and styles of worship. They are against rock-and-roll music and things that are deemed worldly or materialistic. (Photograph courtesy of the Southwest Virginia Historical and Preservation Society.)

Five

PEOPLE AND PLACES

UNCLE DAN TICKLE. Dan Tickle (foreground) served as woods superintendent at the Big Branch camp at the mouth of George Fork on Pound River in 1930. From left to right are (in the background) C. O. Triplett, Dee McKinney, and Dave and Ernie Tickle; (on the walkway) Audrey McKinney and Hazel Triplett holding Clark Triplett. Wood camps were accessible by the company's narrow-gauge railroads. There were gasoline motorcars for the superintendents. The people lived in a time that showed force of character, when nothing was a guarantee from day to day. The basic means of survival required strength and persistence on a daily basis, which was something these people had in abundance. They survived, built homes, raised families, paid their bills and taxes, went to church, and had an unshakable faith in God. (Photograph courtesy of Dennis Reedy.)

THE STANLEY BROTHERS. From left to right are Pee Wee Lambert, Leslie Keith, and Carter and Ralph Stanley in the early 1940s. They played the ballads that were brought from England to the southern Appalachian Mountains, where for centuries they were passed from father to son. (Photograph courtesy of Dennis Reedy.)

THE CONVICT CAMP. This photograph depicts the convict camp on site of the lumberyard at the mouth of Caney Creek in the early 1950s. The land and houses at Fremont went to the Clinchfield Coal Corporation. The towns were divided into 120 lots and sold at auction by the Johnson Land Company. The area that had been the McClure band mill became the convict camp. (Photograph courtesy of Dennis Reedy.)

SWIMMING ON CANEY CREEK. The old swimming hole near the mouth of Caney Creek is pictured in 1929. A portion of Caney yard can be seen in the background. Unlike children of today, children of the 1920s had limited forms of entertainment and had to find ways to amuse themselves. They invented games to play. (Photograph courtesy of Dennis Reedy.)

COMPANY STORE FLOODING. One of the W. M. Ritter Lumber Company stores is seen after the 1957 flood. Notice the overturned building on the left and pumps and hoses in the road. Floods and fires were a common worry for the company officials as well as the residents of camp towns. The people were used to the floods and the destruction that followed them. (Photograph courtesy of Dennis Reedy.)

Lunchtime on Lick Creek. The Lick Creek camp crew takes lunchtime in 1923. W. M. Ritter Lumber Company was known for having good cooks who always prepared plenty of food for workers. The cooks would start about 3:45 a.m. in order to have the breakfast meal prepared at 6:00 a.m. Bacon, sausage, eggs, biscuits, preserves, and coffee were served on two large tables in the dining room. Dinner and supper meals consisted of beans, potatoes, cabbage or slaw, corn bread, pork or other meats, and pies. The cook received a salary of $25 a month. Immediately after breakfast, the cook and one helper would start dinner, which was served from 11:00 to 12:00. If all went well, they might get to rest about 30 minutes or an hour while dinner was served. If a cutting crew couldn't leave the job site, then dinner was taken to them. (Photograph courtesy of Dennis Reedy.)

SUPERVISOR OF STORES. Giles Fink, supervisor of stores, sits on the steps of the company store conversing with Mrs. Don (Elizabeth) Weaver at Fremont around 1939. He recalled how he had started as a drag man and quickly advanced. He often related that if a moonshine still was found in operation, the cutting crew pulled back, no matter how many good logs had to be left. (Photograph courtesy of Dennis Reedy.)

THE TRAMMEL CLUBHOUSE. This picture of Trammel shows the company store, clubhouses, residences, and the boardinghouse. W. M. Ritter had a reputation for good food and clean boardinghouses for out-of-town people traveling by train to the area. The company store, clubhouse, and boardinghouses were a necessary part of camp life. (Photograph courtesy of Dennis Reedy.)

CHICKENS FOR DINNER. Hattie Hall (left) and Nita Ratliff prepare chickens for dinner. Nita Ratliff started working for Ritter in the Caney camp boardinghouse in the 1940s. She helped cook for about 100 men. She prepared three meals a day—breakfast, dinner, and supper at the camp, with carryout lunch for the men that were at cutting sites. (Photograph courtesy of Dennis Reedy.)

NOAH THE TEAMSTER. Noah Tiller, pictured around 1927, was born in the Duty, Virginia, area and received his education in the public schools. In 1908, he started working for the Honaker Lumber Company as a teamster and was later promoted to camp foreman. When the Honaker Company sold out, Noah went to work for Ritter as a skidder foreman on Lick Creek. (Photograph courtesy of Dennis Reedy.)

FREMONT AROUND 1920. As late as 1915, a topographical map of the county produced by the State of Virginia Geological Survey showed no village named McClure and only six houses in the vicinity of the town. The map did not show the McClure River, formerly known as McClure Creek. Legend says the town was named for an early explorer to the area. Fremont was the first of the Ritter Company's operations to be constructed in the county. Work began in 1916 with the clearing of laurel thicket for the sawmill, and the first lumber was produced in early 1917. In addition to the mill, the Fremont community contained about 75 residences, a combination store and office, a post office, a hotel, a community building, a school, and a railway station. It was named for John C. Fremont, a candidate for the presidency in 1856 who was employed as a surveyor on one of the small lines that became part of Clinchfield. (Photograph courtesy of Dennis Reedy.)

HURLEY IN 1928. The Hurley mill and community is pictured in 1928. Hurley was part of the third division of the four W. M. Ritter Lumber Company sawmills and considered the safest of the mills in that area, unlike the Lower Elk mill—around 1930, the roof of the planing mill fell in, injuring 11 workers, some seriously. The injured were loaded on a flat car and taken to the company hospital. (Photograph courtesy of Dennis Reedy.)

IRON MAN FULLER. Claude "Iron Man" Fuller played for No. 9 Mine in Clinchco, Virginia. He never missed a shift of work and would often work two shifts a day, thus the name "Iron Man." He signed with the New York Yankees for $168 per week and played six weeks of minor-league baseball. (Photograph courtesy of Dennis Reedy.)

McClure at Noon. The McClure Hotel is seen here along with the sheds for storing flooring and planing-mill stock. This photograph was taken just before the noon whistle had blown. There were usually about 20 to 30 boarders in the 20-room hotel to cook for. The whistle system was used as a means of telling everyone what time it was. (Photograph courtesy of Dennis Reedy.)

Willie at Work. The log Willie Ratliff sits on measures 16 feet by 35 inches and contains 882 board feet of lumber. The company preferred 80 percent of their logs to be 14 to 16 feet long. The largest log in a tree was the one cut at the stumps just above the ground. It was called the butt cut. (Photograph courtesy of Dennis Reedy.)

RITTER CAMP SPORTS. This early Fremont basketball team in the early 1950s is, from left to right, (first row) Fred Herndon, Lloyd Rose, Kent Chapman, Bill Breese, and Slick Carlton; (second row) Danny Hale, Bill Carlton, Bobby Dingus, Ray Reedy, Charles Breese, and Arthur Lambert. Basketball played an important role in community life in Fremont during the 1950s. Company officials took the sports very seriously. Baseball teams and basketball teams were started in the camps as entertainment. People were hired and fired based on their sports abilities. The companies provided transportation to and from the games. They brought in college players in an attempt to beat the competition. The teams were very difficult to beat, as both teams were in good physical shape considering the jobs they held. (Photograph courtesy of Dennis Reedy.)

THE RITTER FAMILIES. These are members of the various families that lived and worked for the W. M. Ritter Lumber Company at Frying Pan camp in the early 1920s. Those who are identified are (standing) Stella Triplett (second from left, in apron), Mattie Rose (third from left), Ona Breeding (fourth from left), and Charles Triplett holding son Archie (far right); (seated from left to right) Maude Rich, Alma Hinkle, Mag Taylor, Della Chambers, and Lorina Triplett. (Photograph courtesy of Dennis Reedy.)

CABIN FORK CHICKENS. Youngsters had various chores like feeding chickens at the camp on Cabin Fork of Frying Pan Creek. Families lived in the wood camps rent free. Supplies were hauled to the store and boardinghouse regularly by boxcar. Meals were prepared for 50 or more men. A bell located at the kitchen door was rung when a meal was ready. (Photograph courtesy of Dennis Reedy.)

THE FREMONT CLUBHOUSE. The clubhouse at Fremont is seen as it appeared around 1922. Hotels or boardinghouses at Fremont and McClure were more often referred to as clubhouses than hotels. There was only one clubhouse at Fremont. It fed hundreds of hungry workers for nearly 30 years. The meals were prepared by a Native American, black, or white cook. (Photograph courtesy of Dennis Reedy.)

McCLURE'S OLD POST OFFICE. This photograph depicts the building that served as the McClure Post Office after it was moved from the company store. When this facility was constructed, the McClure Post Office was established with Giles J. Fink as postmaster on November 18, 1919. Fink, like many Ritter employees, had several jobs during the course of his career with Ritter. (Photograph courtesy of Dennis Reedy.)

AMERICAN LOG LOADER. From left to right are Lum Moore and Dick Dutton, tong hookers; Palton Moore, loader man; and Asa Bartley, top loader man, in Big Branch Woods in 1929 with the American log loader. The American log loader was made by the American Hoist and Derrick Company. The log loader had the ability to swing. The first use of this loader appears to be about 1929. In 1892, the American Manufacturing Company became the American Hoist and Derrick Company. The American log loader changed the way logs were cut. The early mills had depended on water transportation to ship logs to the mills. They would tie the logs together to form rafts to float them downstream to the sawmill. Then railroads came along and built their own rail lines, often called dummy lines, to get the logs to the mill. (Photograph courtesy of Dennis Reedy.)

DAN THE RAILROAD MAN. Dan Tickle, pictured around 1927, got his first job with the Norfolk and Western Railway Company in 1890 on the section crew as a reward for flagging a passenger train and preventing a serious wreck. In 1895, Tickle went to work for Ritter Lumber Company. He quickly advanced from yard foreman to assistant superintendent. (Photograph courtesy of Dennis Reedy.)

THE SILAS DEELS. Silas and Ethel Deel are pictured on their 51st wedding anniversary. They had 52 grandchildren and 33 great-grandchildren. Silas Deel started working at Squirrel Camp between Clinchco and Fremont. He helped put up the steel at Big Branch and later worked at McClure Woods. The track crew worked hard and generally received low wages. (Photograph courtesy of Dennis Reedy.)

BLOCK OF HEMLOCK. Noah Tiller and his saddle horse are seen on a large block of hemlock. In the early 1900s, Ritter left huge amounts of hemlock in the forest, since no market existed for it at that time. Later it became a desirable material because of lasting quality and resistance to termites. Ritter lost several million feet of this timber. (Photograph courtesy of Dennis Reedy.)

DRY LUMBER LOADING. Inspector ? Smith and a crew load dry lumber for shipping. Different species of tree such as oak, maple, poplar, beech, and others are kiln-dried on different schedules set up by the Forest Products Laboratory according to the moisture content of the wood. Moisture content is scheduled by cutting a one-inch section of the board and weighing the sample. (Photograph courtesy of Dennis Reedy.)

SWAMPY CYPRESS LOGS. Logging was difficult no matter the area it was cut in, but no area was as difficult as the river swamps. This log is from the Collecton Cypress Company. In addition to cypress, the Cypress Company also cut gum from the swampy areas in South Carolina and Georgia. Ritter wanted to see if his business could succeed in different areas and climates. He and his associates had to build several railroads to reach timber holdings and to get them to the sawmill plants. Most of the early sawmills were circular mills, operating only two to five years at a particular location from 1890 to 1905. In 1899 at Dry Fork (also known as Ritter and Avondale), band saws were introduced. This marked a new development in Ritter's type of manufacture, and therefore the mills were fewer but larger. (Photograph courtesy of Dennis Reedy.)

Six

INDUSTRY

THE HARDWOOD BARK MAGAZINE. The *Hardwood Bark* and *Red Jacketeer* magazines were published by the Ritter Lumber Company and given free to its employees. These magazines contained pictures and news items from all of Ritter's operations as well as jokes and items of general interest to the lumber industry. *Hardwood Bark*s contained 22 to 28 pages and measured about 7.75 by 10.5 inches. Ritter Lumber Company dominated the industry in the county and changed life in the county by opening the area up with its logging and railroad operations. Ritter provided jobs from 1890 until 1929. From 1929 until the late 1980s, Clinchfield Coal Company would be the major source of employment. The county is changing in an attempt to capitalize on the tourism industry. (Photograph courtesy of Dennis Reedy.)

POPLAR LOGS AT BANDY. A great deal of poplar and basswood was stacked high on the hill at Fremont and McClure. This enabled the lumberyards to be larger and provided better air circulation for the wood, which reduced the chances of sap staining. (Photograph courtesy of Dennis Reedy.)

MINERS AT WORK. Ritter Lumber Company mined coal to supply its own needs—for the homes, offices, and buildings of the company. The coal mine had been owned by the Clinchfield Coal Corporation and leased to Ritter. The mine was located one mile north of Fremont. It usually employed about 14 men. (Photograph courtesy of Dennis Reedy.)

AMUSEMENTS FOR THE CAMPS. Von Shores and his airplane, a Waco with air-cooled Warner-Scarch radical engine, rest at the landing field along the Powell River at Big Sandy Gap around 1930. Holders of these photographs were entitled to one free chance to win the airplane in the photograph after 1,600 of those photographs were sold. (Photograph courtesy of Dennis Reedy.)

MIDDLETOWN BLACK WORKERS. This group of railroad workers in the early 1920s lived in a group of houses between Fremont and McClure known as Middletown. When McClure was built, blacks lived at Middletown, and the area was commonly called Colored Town. The blacks were completely segregated from the white community. They were run out of town around 1930. (Photograph courtesy of Dennis Reedy.)

DRAY WAGON WORKERS. Bob Laws and Homer Barrett ride in the dray wagon at Fremont. Delivery vehicles, whether wagon or truck, were referred to as drays. A truck replaced the dray wagon at McClure around 1930. A one-horse wagon was used at Fremont until the operation closed around 1939. At Fremont, the dray met the train and hauled the mail. (Photograph courtesy of Dennis Reedy.)

SHAY NO. 949. The Shay engine No. 949 had pinion gears. A slip joint for expansion of the driveline and a universal joint for bending of the shaft can be seen to the right of the wheels just under the cab steps. The Shays used in the county weighed between 36 and 42 tons. (Photograph courtesy of Dennis Reedy.)

THE MCCLURE BRIDGE. The railroad built across McClure River in 1927 led to the Caney yard. In addition to the large bridge across the McClure River at Fremont, spans of unique construction were also built across Cranes Nest, Pound, and Russell Fork Rivers. To accommodate a large flow of water, such bridges required the use of piers instead of wooden timbers. (Photograph courtesy of Dennis Reedy.)

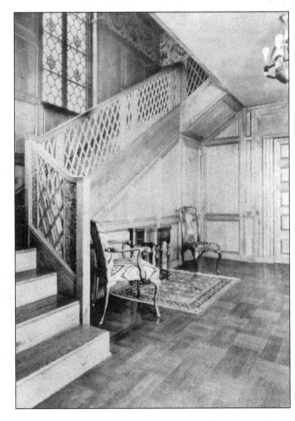

RITTER'S FAMOUS FLOORING. This house had Ritter parquet flooring laid in the basket-weave design. The parquet flooring came in three designs: herringbone, block, and basket weave. Some of the smaller pieces of flooring were glued together or fastened together with metal strips to form blocks. The finished product had a mirror-like shine. (Photograph courtesy of Dennis Reedy.)

RITTER FLOOR ADVERTISEMENT.
This is from the September 1928 issue of *House and Garden* magazine. Ritter gained a worldwide reputation for his quarter-sawn oak parquet flooring. The flooring found its way into some of the finest homes and commercial buildings in the United States and abroad. (Photograph courtesy of Dennis Reedy.)

BIG BRANCH CAMP. The Big Branch camp is not a tourist camp but one that has the look of a trim Methodist summer resort. Notice how clean and neat the camp is. That is due to the diligence of Dan Tickle, the woods superintendent. (Photograph courtesy of Dennis Reedy.)

STEAM ENGINE BRAKEMAN. Rabbit Pittman is pictured with part of a steam engine that ran a band mill. Rabbit was a lifelong Ritter employee starting at the Fremont School. He then went to work at the logging camp above McClure at Stratton as a left-handed spike driver. He would later become a fireman and brakeman on the log train. (Photograph courtesy of Dennis Reedy.)

RITTER PAY STUB. This pay stub is for Lawson Ramsey from the Ritter Lumber Company. Wages were typically low and the hours were usually long. Until organized labor arrived, similar conditions prevailed in the mining industry as well, since mining was the only alternative to the logging jobs. Wages plummeted during the 1930s as the country's economy was crushed in the Depression. (Photograph courtesy of Dennis Reedy.)

MCCLURE LUMBER BUILDERS. The McClure Lumber and Builders Supply occupied this Quonset building in September 1948. In 1951, the old Ritter clubhouse was purchased by the Herndons and they converted part of the building to a store. (Photograph courtesy of Dennis Reedy.)

FRYING PAN CAMP. The employees of the Frying Pan camp are pictured in the 1920s. The county had three large camps: Big Branch, which provided logs for the mill at Fremont; Lick Creek; and Frying Pan. Both Lick Creek and Frying Pan served the McClure mill. Smaller auxiliary camps were constructed as needed. (Photograph courtesy of Dennis Reedy.)

SHAY NO. 19. The Shay No. 19 C/N 1568 carries logs to the mill in 1958. Ritter purchased this engine, a 1905 three-truck standard-gauge of 65 tons, from Elk River Coal and Lumber Company in 1958. The engine worked at Dry Gulch and Tombstone Railroad out of Wytheville, Virginia. (Photograph courtesy of Dennis Reedy.)

PLANT NO. 32. The Plant No. 32 tipple took coal from two separate directions. The coal industry in the county was competitive throughout the world. Plant No. 32 produced more coal than any other coal producer in the area. Ritter mined coal to supply its own needs, and only later did it expand from the lumber to coal industries. (Photograph courtesy of Dennis Reedy.)

CUMBERLAND MOUNTAIN CAMP. C. O. Triplett is seen in the Big Branch camp in the Cumberland Mountains. Life in the wood camps was difficult. Many times, the locomotive engineers accommodated the camp residents by taking them to Fremont or McClure to see the moving pictures or to a ballgame. A boxcar scattered with straw or perhaps a gondola were filled with people for the ride. (Photograph courtesy of Dennis Reedy.)

RITTER CUTTING CREW. The Ritter cutting crew fell a poplar. The crews brought down the monarchs of the forest with crosscut saws and double-bitted axes. As soon as rights to timber had been gained, crews in the woods went to work. First skid roads were built into an area for the teams of horses to pull the logs over. (Photograph courtesy of Dennis Reedy.)

CROSSCUT SAWING CREW. Ezra O'Quinn (left) and Morgan Duty work. Notice the boots and leather leggings and the crosscut saw. Grease was often applied to pole roads on level grades to lessen the resistance of the logs. Timber cutters were paid by board feet in the logs they cut—$1.75 per 1,000 board feet in the early 1930s. (Photograph courtesy of Dennis Reedy.)

PAUL BUNYAN WORKS. Driver Paul Lee is seen with his team on Caney Creek in 1940. Paul was known as "Paul Bunyan." Men like him worked in steep places, where logs would skid too fast to handle. Some places were so steep, rugged, and otherwise inaccessible that horses couldn't be used. Skidders were used instead. A skidder was a steam-driven hoist engine that pulled logs. (Photograph courtesy of Dennis Reedy.)

CANEY CAMP FOREMAN. Noah Tiller, woods superintendent (left), and Luther Crabtree, camp foreman in 1935, are seen with a new team from Ohio. Long manes and tails would be trimmed by blacksmith Frank Fletcher before the horses went to work in the woods. Most horses were bought in Ohio, but some were purchased in Vermont. (Photograph courtesy of Dennis Reedy.)

MOVING 2,500 LOGS. Logs were brought across the ridge between Prater Creek and the Tilda Anderson Branch of the Russell Fork with teams, tractor, and the Lidgewood skidder by the Frying Pan crews. When this photograph was taken, Sam Counts and his crew had just completed a logging railroad to these logs. (Photograph courtesy of Dennis Reedy.)

THE AMERICAN LOG LOADER. The American log loader crew poses. Log cars did not run underneath the American log loader. Instead it swung around, picked up an empty car, and set it ahead for loading, working through the entire trip in this manner. Sometimes the log cars were set off to the side of the track if there was room. (Photograph courtesy of Dennis Reedy.)

MCCLURE SAWMILL. The McClure pond is filled with logs and lumber waiting to be staked in this 1925 scene of the McClure mill during its peak of operations. The sawmill was a large two-story affair. The head saw, edger, trimmer, and other machinery used in the actual production of the lumber were located on the second floor. (Photograph courtesy of Dennis Reedy.)

THE FREMONT MILL. The Fremont mill is seen as it appeared around 1920. Ritter Lumber's dimension mills supplied a new breed of companies. One interesting customer of yellow poplar and basswood dimensions was A. I. Root Manufacturing Company of Medina, Ohio, said to be the largest producer of beekeeper supplies. A lot of the poplar dimension was used to make washboards. (Photograph courtesy of Dennis Reedy.)

COUNTS RAILROAD CREW. The Sam Counts railroad crew works on the railroad track. From left to right are Paul Selfe, Homer Harlow, Sam Counts, Dave Silcox, Will Bostic, Garland Yates, Starlin Duty, Dock Bostic, and Tom Owens. The actual laying of track was done by hand. It was back-breaking manual labor. (Photograph courtesy of Dennis Reedy.)

MITCHELL BRANCH TIPPLE. The No. 32 tipple and company houses were along Mitchell Branch. Note the wooden railway cars laden with coal. The bulk of coal operations, with a capacity of 8,000 tons per day, were located at Red Jacket on the main line of the Norfolk and Western Railroad. (Photograph courtesy of Dennis Reedy.)

FIREMAN AND BRAKEMAN. Deward Presley (left) was fireman and John Henry Nickels (right) was brakeman for engineer Bill Fletcher on the Big 1 on Caney about 1940. John Henry started working for Ritter as a tong hooker and worked over 48 years for the company. He worked at Blackey, McClure, Race Fork, New River, and Coal Mountain. (Photograph courtesy of Dennis Reedy.)

THE CARPENTER CREW AROUND 1949. From left to right are Jeno Stapleton, Leonard Stanley, Jack Fields, Ray Conley, and Rice Fields. Rice, or C. R. as he was known, helped build the houses, store, boardinghouses, mill, and lumberyards for W. M. Ritter. He also worked at the McClure planing mill when he wasn't needed elsewhere. (Photograph courtesy of Dennis Reedy.)

LITTLE ONE ENGINE. Arthur Patton pauses for a smoke in the "Little One." The engineer had the best job of any railroad worker. When operating the train, he was always seated inside out of the weather. Engineers usually started out as brakemen. The routes taken by Ritter's railroads through the county were many. In the 1930s, the line was extended. (Photograph courtesy of Dennis Reedy.)

Seven

PITTSTON V. UMWA
STRIKE

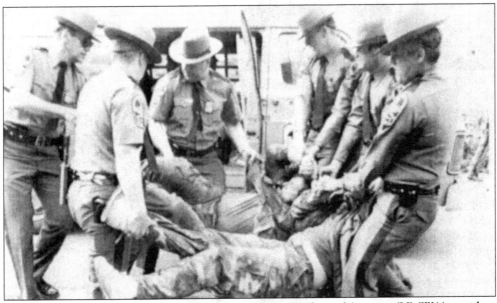

PITTSTON V. UMWA. On April 5, 1989, United Mine Workers of America (UMWA) president Richard L. Trumka announced that the miners were striking against Pittston Coal Group and its corporate parent, the Pittston Company, over allegations of unfair labor practices. The coal miners had worked 14 months without a contract at Pittston Coal Group mines. The 1,700 UMWA members in three states said they were striking for job security and medical benefits. Pittston said it needed flexibility to stay competitive in world coal markets as an exporter of coal for steel making. The company began hiring replacement workers as soon as the miners walked off their jobs. The battle that started between Pittston Group and the miners would result in U.S. marshals and state police struggling to maintain order. Judges on the state and federal level would be the ultimate authority in settling the strike after millions of dollars in fines had been imposed against the union. (Photograph courtesy of the *Dickenson Star*.)

Gov. Gerald Baliles. Gov. Gerald Baliles was governor of Virginia during the Pittston v. UMWA strike. The governors of Virginia, Kentucky, and West Virginia had agreed not to intervene in the strike. The governors had asked for a 30- to 60-day cooling-off period. The union delayed the strike until April 5, 1989, based on that request. (Photograph courtesy of the *Dickenson Star*.)

Federal Judge Becomes a Mediator. Federal judge Glen Williams was responsible for bringing the union and Pittston Coal Group together in an attempt to resume bargaining talks. Judge Williams called both sides to the meeting in an effort to restore some normalcy. Judge Williams became concerned when union members defied his court order to stop civil disobedience. (Photograph courtesy of the *Dickenson Star*.)

JUDGE DONALD MCGLOTHLIN JR.
Russell County Circuit Court judge Donald McGlothlin Jr. handed down large fines against the UMWA. The fines would eventually reach over $64 million. Much of that would be reduced. But his father, Donald Sr., would lose his 4th District House seat to Jackie Stump, one of the UMWA officials, as a result of the strike. (Photograph courtesy of the *Dickenson Star*.)

UMWA PRESIDENT TRUMKA.
Richard L. Trumka, the UMWA president, called for the strike against Pittston on April 5, 1989. The strike was a result of a 14-month conflict that had dominated the news in the coalfields of Southwest Virginia. Both sides had pushed their agenda to the public, circulating advertisements and booklets on their respective positions. (Photograph courtesy of the *Dickenson Star*.)

UNITED WE STAND. The scene of Virginia state police and striking miners became common during the many months of the strike. The state police were called in to handle the "dirty work" of the strike. They had a difficult job of maintaining order during a strike that would include riots, bombs placed at a Pittston warehouse, shots fired at trucks, and general unrest. (Photograph courtesy of the *Dickenson Star.*)

COMMITTED TO A CAUSE. The scene of coal miners being handcuffed became common during 1989–1990. Three weeks into the strike, over 200 miners had been arrested. They were taken to the Dickenson County jail, where those giving fictitious names of John Doe were jailed and those giving their actual names were released. (Photograph courtesy of the *Dickenson Star.*)

ARRESTS ARE MADE. Mass arrests were made of striking union miners for blocking entrances to Pittston Coal Group operations. The Virginia State Police reported that arrests included Jackie Stump, District 28 president; members of the Daughters of Mother Jones, an organization of miners' and pensioners' wives, were arrested at Moss No. 3 preparation plant. (Photograph courtesy of the *Dickenson Star*.)

DEMAND FOR SUPPORT. As the strike stretched into months, the people demanded support from Congressman Rick Boucher, Sen. Charles S. Robb, and Governor Baliles. Governor Baliles kept his cool during the strike and urged both sides to resume negotiations and call in federal mediators. He made it clear that violence, whether instigated by management or labor, would not be tolerated. (Photograph courtesy of the *Dickenson Star*.)

Labor In America
"We Won't Go Back"

UMWA/Pittston
Strike 1989-90

HEALTH CARE QUESTIONED. The UMWA stated they had received word that Pittston Company had canceled health insurance for sick, injured, and laid-off miners, while company officials claimed only laid-off and active miners lost health-care benefits. Mike Odom, president of Pittston, stated the company continued coverage for the sick and injured miners but did terminate coverage for laid-off personnel. Striking miners were denied coverage. (Photograph courtesy of the *Dickenson Star*.)

SHOTS FIRED AT TRUCK. Tension eased over the Memorial Day holiday in 1989 only to escalate a few days later, when the state police reported that shots had been fired into an occupied coal truck near one of Pittston's operations. Two small-caliber shots were fired into the windshield of the truck near Pittston's Yowling Branch mine. (Photograph courtesy of the *Dickenson Star*.)

REFUSAL TO SERVE. Tempers and emotions ran high in the coalfields, with the merchants refusing to serve the state police, despite the state police's presence in the area as a peacekeeping force. The locals viewed them as hired guns for Pittston and therefore the enemy of the union. The merchants' anger rose when Sister Bernadette Kenny was arrested for allegedly impeding traffic. (Photograph courtesy of the *Dickenson Star*.)

DOUG WILDER VISITS. In a bid to become the first elected black governor in history, Lt. Gov. Doug Wilder challenged his opponent, Marshall Coleman, to visit the coalfields to witness first-hand the effects of the strike on Southwest Virginia. Wilder met with area leaders and UMWA members. (Photograph courtesy of the *Dickenson Star*.)

MINERS ON STRIKE. Striking miners from Kentucky, West Virginia, Indiana, Illinois, Pennsylvania, and Ohio flood the county's back roads in an effort to slow Pittston's coal transportation. Coal group president Mike Odom said in an interview that the influx of people had caused his company to shut down operations for much of that time. (Photograph courtesy of the Dickenson Star.)

STRIKE IS SETTLED. On February 20, 1990, the bitter 14-month-old labor strike ended. UMWA leaders made it official that 63 percent of the workers had ratified a contract settlement between Pittston and the union. "We are thrilled. It's a joyous day for everyone involved," U.S. secretary of labor Elizabeth Dole said. (Photograph courtesy of the *Dickenson Star.*)

Eight

PRESENT DAY

CARTER MUSICAL MARKER. Since 84 percent of Dickenson County's area is woodland, mining and lumber are still the primary employers, and farming is still performed on a small scale. What one identifies with the county is its musical legends. As the marker shows, the Carter Family was prominent throughout Scott, Dickenson, and Wise Counties. They are commonly called the "First Family of Country Music." The members included A. P., Sara, and Maybelle Carter. Their first recording session took place in Bristol for the Victor Talking Machine Company in 1927. The major industry besides farming and mining is tourism. The Breaks Interstate Park and the John Flannagan Dam provide unlimited possibilities for the outdoor enthusiast. The Ralph Stanley Museum and yearly festival provide music lovers with an insight into Ralph Stanley's beginnings in the mountains of Dickenson County. (Photograph courtesy of the Southwest Virginia Historical and Preservation Society.)

RALPH STANLEY MUSEUM. The house that is now the Ralph Stanley Museum was built by Sen. Roland Chase around 1903. It was the first brick house in Clintwood. Roland's father, Capt. John P. Chase, a founder of Clintwood, gave the adjoining land for the Dickenson County courthouse. The senator's law practice was on the ground level. (Photograph courtesy of the Southwest Virginia Historical and Preservation Society.)

DICKENSON COUNTY FAIR. The Dickenson County Fair was a yearly event and widely anticipated, as agriculture in the county consists of small-scale, part-time farms with 10,000 acres in use. Some tobacco crops and forage are produced near the rivers. There are also 800 head of horses, primarily used for entertainment and horse shows. (Photograph courtesy of Dennis Reedy.)

JOHN FLANNAGAN DAM. The John Flannagan Dam is quite large and is part of the Big Sandy River flood protection system. The dam is named after Congressman John W. Flannagan, commonly known as the "Clintwood Cyclone." Flannagan served the Ninth Congressional District from 1931 until 1949, when he retired. The dam was completed in 1964. (Photograph courtesy of the Southwest Virginia Historical and Preservation Society.)

THE BREAKS PARK. The Breaks Interstate Park is commonly referred to as the "Grand Canyon of the South." Yearly thousands seek the beauty of the cliffs and trails. Many enjoy the amazing bird watching and rafting that is available at the park. The conference center and amphitheater make it possible for conferences to be held in the beautiful environment. (Photograph courtesy of the Southwest Virginia Historical and Preservation Society.)

CLINCHFIELD COAL COMPANY. Shown is one of the Clinchfield Coal Company warehouses located in the county. Clinchfield Coal built much of the area when it was at its peak during the mining boom. They still have some business interests in the area. However, tourism is now the main source of additional revenue and is becoming the major employer among the developing industries. (Photograph courtesy of the Southwest Virginia Historical and Preservation Society.)

THE LAST SPIKE. Trammel, Virginia, is where George L. Carter drove the last spike on behalf of the CC&O Railroad. This reenactment took place in 1990. The CC&O started in 1913. Passenger service was available shortly after. With the railroad available, the coal industry could thrive, and since then, coal has served as the major employer. (Photograph courtesy of Dennis Reedy.)

BIRCH KNOB TOWER AND OBSERVATION POINT. With an elevation of 4,162 feet, the tower is one of the area's most sought-after tourism sights. Most people at some point during hiking and sightseeing make it to see the tower high on Birch Knob in Dickenson County. (Photograph courtesy of Dennis Reedy.)

JETTIE BAKER CENTER. The Jettie Baker Center—formerly known as the Mullins Theater—was built in the 1940s. It was donated to the town of Clintwood by Mrs. Jettie Baker. The property has been completely renovated and hosts a number of talented performers. It will seat 350 comfortably. (Photograph courtesy of the Southwest Virginia Historical and Preservation Society.)

BIBLIOGRAPHY

Reedy, Dennis. *The W. M. Ritter Lumber Company—Family History Book*. Clinchco, VA: Dennis E. Reedy, 1983.

Reedy, Dennis and Diana. *Haysi, Virginia, Community and Family History*. Clinchco, VA: Dennis and Diana Reedy, 1998.

Reedy, Dennis, ed. *Schools and Community History of Dickenson County, Virginia*. Johnson City, TN: The Overmountain Press, 1992.

Goforth, James. *Building the Clinchfield*. Erwin, TN: Gem Publishers, 1989.

"Labor In America—We Won't Go Back." *The Dickenson Star*. Clinchco, Virginia: 1990.

INDEX

DISCOVER THOUSANDS OF LOCAL HISTORY BOOKS FEATURING MILLIONS OF VINTAGE IMAGES

Arcadia Publishing, the leading local history publisher in the United States, is committed to making history accessible and meaningful through publishing books that celebrate and preserve the heritage of America's people and places.

Find more books like this at
www.arcadiapublishing.com

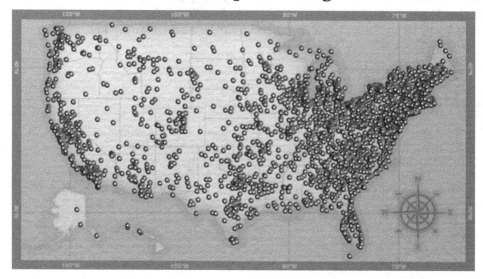

Search for your hometown history, your old stomping grounds, and even your favorite sports team.

Consistent with our mission to preserve history on a local level, this book was printed in South Carolina on American-made paper and manufactured entirely in the United States. Products carrying the accredited Forest Stewardship Council (FSC) label are printed on 100 percent FSC-certified paper.

MADE IN THE USA

CPSIA information can be obtained
at www.ICGtesting.com
Printed in the USA
LVHW061143190723
752798LV00009B/715

IMAGES
of America

FAIRHOPE

Looking to the Bay — Colonial Inn —

The 1909 Colonial Inn commanded a superb view of Mobile Bay. The inn, razed in the 1990s, was a dining and social center in the village of Fairhope, which became a popular winter resort. The hotel that hosted visitors from across the country for decades was wrapped in spacious porches to catch the soft summertime Gulf breezes. (Courtesy Debbie Quinn.)

On the cover: Barefoot children enjoy the cool waters of Sweetwater Branch on the bay near Fairhope. The stream served as a source of fresh water for the settlement before the community well was put down in front of the colony general store. Even after that, old-timers remember trips to the branch as children when they rode on wagons with barrels to get sweet drinking water.

IMAGES
of America

FAIRHOPE

Cathy Donelson
With foreword by Fannie Flagg

ARCADIA
PUBLISHING

Published by Arcadia Publishing
Charleston, South Carolina

Library of Congress Catalog Card Number: 2005931515

For all general information contact Arcadia Publishing at:
Telephone 843-853-2070
Fax 843-853-0044
E-mail sales@arcadiapublishing.com
For customer service and orders:
Toll-Free 1-888-313-2665

Visit us on the Internet at www.arcadiapublishing.com

The bluff overlooking Mobile Bay remains as much of a landmark today as it was when the first expeditions of conquistadors and European explorers sailed into the bay in search of a new world and treasure. One treasure they found turned out to be a world-class waterfront view in one of the most unusual small towns in America.

CONTENTS

FOREWORD

Nothing pleases me more than to be asked to write about Fairhope. I hope that after you read this marvelous book, you too will agree that Fairhope is a special place, with a unique history and an even more exciting future.

Perched high on a bluff, overlooking the beautiful Mobile Bay, Fairhope seems, to those of us who love it, just like Utopia. Not surprising, the town was founded by a group of people known as "The Utopians." Since then, Fairhope has gone on to become a haven to many artists and writers who have gathered here from all over the world and now make it their home. As they have found out, you can travel far and wide and not find a more perfect little town, and once you have been here, I promise you, you will never forget it.

I can still remember that summer evening in 1955 (long before the interstate freeway), when my family and I, headed for Gulf Shores, drove through Fairhope for the first time on old Highway 98. I was completely mesmerized by the magical look of the place—the lights in the trees casting dancing shadows on the ground as the Spanish moss blew gently in the warm breeze, the smell of the night blooming jasmine, the twinkling lights of Mobile sparkling like a jeweled necklace across the bay.

One look and Fairhope cast her spell on me. That night, I made a secret vow that one day I would return, and return I did. And now so many years later, whenever work or some other such foolishness, calls me away for too long, I find that secret invisible thread begins to pull at my heartstrings calling me back home.

You may very well wonder what it is about this place that affects all of us who love it so. I have asked myself that same question a hundred times. Is it the friendly people? The closeness of the community? The unique downtown shops, the delicious seafood? Or could it be the serene beauty and calmness of the bay, the fragrance of the wild honeysuckle, wisteria, and gardenia blooming in spring?

Is it the hundreds of majestic oak trees with Spanish moss hanging from every limb, or the tall pine and cedar trees that can be found all over town? Or the beautiful historic old homes that line the boardwalk by the Grand Hotel? The little Orange Street pier? The colorful sailboats across the water on a bright sunny day? The warm balmy winters when on Christmas day, more often than not, folks walk around in their shirtsleeves while our northern neighbors shovel snow?

Is it the large array of birds—red birds, blue birds, snowy-white egrets, blue heron, pelicans, and sea gulls—that live here year-round? The many parks where one can safely walk night and day? Is it the Art Walk all over town? The great bookstores? The fresh flowers that line every street? The outdoor band concerts in summer? Or could it simply be the magnificent sunsets on the bay every evening? The answer is yes, all this and much more.

Although I've done my best to describe it, the truth is, Fairhope is really a state of mind and cannot be explained by using mere words. It must be felt. So I'm giving you fair warning. Visitors and tourists beware: if you come here, you, too, just might fall in love with Fairhope and stay forever.

—Fannie Flagg

INTRODUCTION

Long before the English humanist and statesman Sir Thomas More published his *Utopia* in 1516, man dreamed of finding or establishing a perfect place.

Fairhope, a small town that has played a large role in American history, is the result of those kinds of dreams. The site of the model community founded from scratch on Alabama's Gulf Coast by visionaries in 1894 had been imagined as an ideal location for a city by many others before them.

Vintage views of the remarkable colony created out of their vision of a Utopian society are presented in the pages of this book, which conveys a special sense of time and place.

Utopia means "no place" in Greek. Ironically the founders of Fairhope had selected the name of their experimental colony in the late 19th century before they decided on a place for the town they thought would have a "fair hope" of succeeding.

Idealists and freethinkers from across the country who were devoted to the economic theory of a single tax on land pooled their resources to create an intentional community to demonstrate their ideals. They cast their fortunes and futures upon a forested bluff with a sweeping and panoramic view of the bay for their communal colony based on a concept of "cooperative individualism."

From the beginning of European exploration of the Gulf of Mexico, the inviting bluff on the Eastern Shore of the bay was part of a struggle for a New World empire. Spain first claimed the scenic region that early conquistadors believed held a fabled fountain of youth.

Alonso Alvarez de Pineda, an explorer who had sailed with Christopher Columbus, was the first to map the bay in 1519. Laying claim to the region for Spain, he named the bay Espiritu Santo, or Bay of the Holy Spirit.

Despite Spanish efforts to hold title to the lush stretch of semi-tropical coastline, it was the French who established a permanent settlement there. A colonization expedition sent by Louis XIV, the flamboyant Sun King, landed on a Gulf beach south of the future site of Fairhope in 1699 and built a fort upriver.

Mobile was established in 1711 and became the capital of old Louisiana, named in honor of King Louis. French plantations to supply the colony were located on the bluffs across the bay.

Two Canadian brothers, Jean Baptiste le Moyne, sieur de Bienville, and Pierre, sieur d'Iberville, led the expedition to settle the area to squeeze the rival British out of the Atlantic Coast where they had founded colonies.

In 1703, d'Iberville was named the first governor of French Louisiana. He asked the king for a grant of land around Mobile Bay, including the great bluffs on the Eastern Shore, but the crown refused. The rich land was intended to attract settlers from France.

D'Iberville's tenure as governor was short-lived. He died in Havana in 1706 while planning an invasion to drive the English from the Eastern Seaboard. If the plan had succeeded, it would have changed the course of American history.

The first recorded settler may not have arrived willingly at what is now Fairhope. Pierre Laurendine, a 21-year-old soldier, arrived in the Louisiana colony in 1727 on a ship listing its passengers as "Deserters and Others Sent by Order of the King."

He became a landowner and established a plantation on the Eastern Shore. After his death in 1769, his holdings passed to his son Jean Baptiste Laurendine.

Old Louisiana was dismembered after the Peace of Paris in 1763, when part of the area passed to Britain, essentially becoming a 14th colony, British West Florida. The two leading British officials of the province established plantations on prime lands north and south of Laurendine and laid out a new town there to supplant Mobile.

However, the Revolutionary War scuttled plans for their dream town on the Eastern Shore. In 1779, the British surrendered the area to Spanish forces.

In 1800, Laurendine, calling himself "an old inhabitant of this District," petitioned the Spanish commandant at Mobile for pastureland across the bay because, he said, an Appalachee tribe uprising placed him at risk of losing his cattle.

His request was granted, and in 1805, Laurendine sold his land, which also contained a house and kitchen, for $120 to Louis de Feriet of New Orleans. The French baron was a lieutenant with a Spanish regiment of Louisiana Infantry serving in Mobile.

The rest is history, illustrated by maps, drawings, and photographs contained in this book. The images tell the story of still another dream town, Alabama City, which was platted on the bluff. But yet another conflict, the Civil War, intervened. The site of Fairhope remained pine and pastureland until the so-called "single-taxers" arrived to create their model town.

Their creation became the oldest and largest single-tax colony in the world and the most successful.

The unique village drew progressives and Populists, Socialists and Quakers, artists and intellectuals, and even nudists and free-love advocates. Many of the major social reformers of the early 20th century—from Dewey to Darrow—made pilgrimages to Fairhope. Strong individualists, fine minds, independent spirits, and colorful characters of all sorts came to inhabit the town founded on principle.

Thanks go to all who treasure the mystique and magic of "Old Fairhope," especially those who shared their historic documents and heirloom photographs along with their memories of some of its forgotten people and places.

One

UTOPIAN DREAMS

The second matter that I take the liberty of communicating to Your Lordship is the advantages that will accrue to the Province of establishing a Town on the East side of the Bay of Mobile, below a place called the Red Cliffs, as the unhealthy Situation of the present one makes such a measure necessary.

—Elias Walker Durnford, acting governor,
British West Florida, February 3, 1770

Fairhope hugs the Eastern Shore of Mobile Bay, where English officials envisioned a new seat of government to supplant the old Colonial capital of Mobile, a fever-ridden bone yard for British troops. Laid out with streets at oblique angles to take advantage of the fresh bay winds, this visionary town remained a dream.

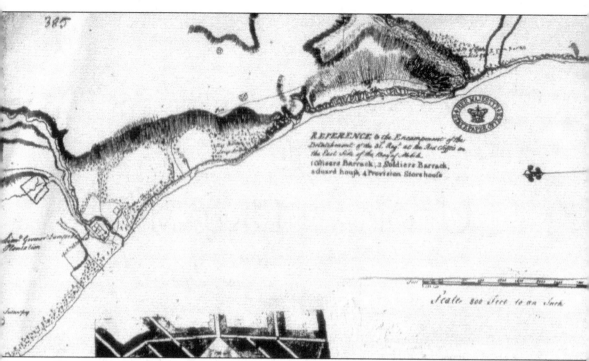

Elias Walker Durnford, royal surveyor and governor of British West Florida from 1769 to 1780, proposed a town where Fairhope lies today. Durnford and Edmund Rush Weggs, the attorney general of the province and owner of the plantation shown at the right of the drawing, offered to give up some of their Eastern Shore holdings for a town to replace Mobile. Durnford owned

Creole descendants of the old French Louisiana founders first settled the Fairhope bay front. Martha Juzang (right) and daughter Olivet lived in an early settlement on Magnolia Beach where old Creole families still own land. One of their ancestors, Pierre Juzang, was the Spanish crown's commissary for American Indians in Mobile. He received one of Spain's first land grants in the region. (Courtesy Eleanor Harpe.)

10

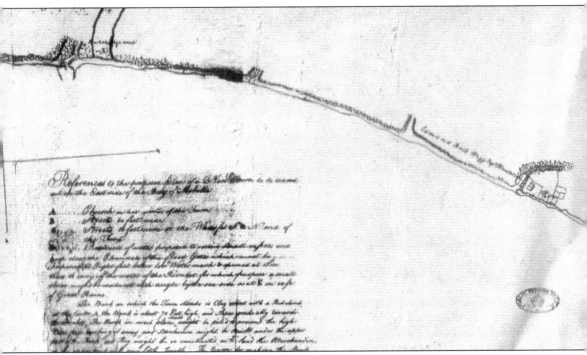

over 57,000 acres along the Gulf Coast, including a 5,000-acre plantation north of Fairhope. The Revolutionary War dashed Britain's hopes of establishing the new city. After the takeover by Spain, this area became part of Spanish West Florida.

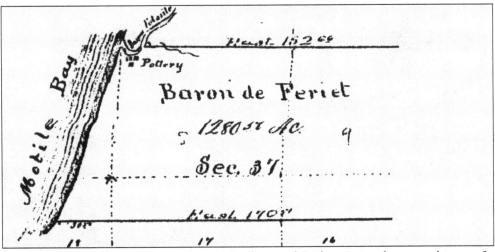

French settler Jean Baptiste Laurendine originally owned Fairhope's site, shown on this map. In 1805, Spain granted his abandoned plantation to Baron Louis de Feriet of New Orleans. De Feriet married the youngest daughter of Gilbert Antoine de St. Maxent, the richest Frenchman in all of old Louisiana, who controlled the trade along the Mississippi River. (Courtesy University of South Alabama Center for Archaeological Studies.)

The historic Jackson Oak still stands in Daphne near Fairhope. Andrew Jackson climbed the legendary landmark in 1814 to rally 3,000 troops to occupy Mobile, thus ending Spanish Colonial rule in the region. "Old Hickory" then moved on to defeat the British in the Battle of New Orleans. What is now Fairhope became American territory for the first time after the War of 1812. (Courtesy Palmer Hamilton.)

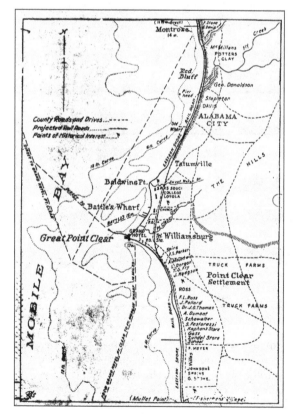

In the 1830s, a group of wealthy speculators headed by famed New Orleans developer Laurent Millaudon next dreamed of a planned town where Fairhope is today. They purchased the de Feriet tract to establish Alabama City. An early map of part of the Baldwin County shoreline not only shows Alabama City, but also indicates an Eastern Shore Railroad, which was never constructed.

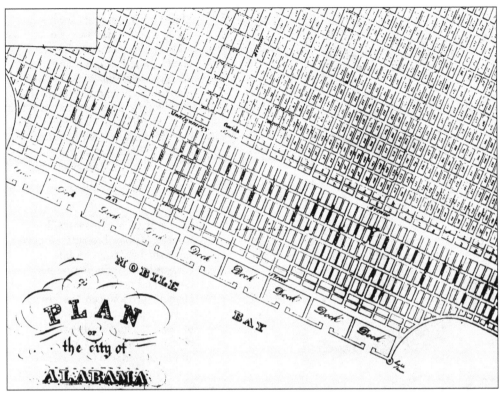

A plat of Alabama City shows a seaport laid out on a plan similar to Savannah, with wharves, named streets, and spacious squares. Several of the 10,000 lots were purchased in sales in Mobile and Montgomery, but the new town that developers hoped would someday rival Mobile across the bay never got off the ground.

In 1858, Congress confirmed Millaudon's claim to the Alabama City property. Years earlier, Congress also had empowered the influential developer to dig a canal on Canal Street in New Orleans. The Civil War defeated his plans for Alabama City, and in the 1870s, Millaudon's heirs sold the Alabama tract to area families in a courthouse sale.

35TH CONGRESS, 1ST SESSION.

S. 81.

[H. Report No. 219.]

IN THE HOUSE OF REPRESENTATIVES

MARCH 26, 1858.

Reported back from the Committee on Private Land Claims without amendment, and committed to a Committee of the Whole House to-morrow.

AN ACT

For the relief of Laurent Millaudon.

1 *Be it enacted by the Senate and House of Representa-*
2 *tives of the United States of America in Congress assembled,*
3 That Laurent Millaudon be, and he is hereby, confirmed in
4 his title to two certain tracts of land lying on the east side
5 of Mobile bay, in the State of Alabama, being the two tracts
6 of land known as the De Feriet claims, as surveyed in the
7 year eighteen hundred and thirty, and approved of by the
8 surveyor general in the year eighteen hundred and thirty-five,
9 with the exception of so much off of the north end thereof as
10 has heretofore been surveyed and confirmed to William Pat-
11 terson, and included within what is known as the Patterson
12 claim, as now located : *Provided,* That this act shall only
13 be construed as a relinquishment of any title that the United
14 States may have to said lands : *And provided, further,* That
15 this confirmation shall enure to the benefit of any other per-

Ellen Hill, a former slave who became one of Fairhope's best-known and most beloved residents, was one of the few people living in the vicinity after Alabama City failed to materialize. She and her family lived on a bluff overlooking the bay at Sea Cliff. Mischievous local youngsters brought chickens they had stolen to "Aunt Ellen" to fry for them. (Courtesy Flora Maye Simmons.)

For many years, the swift side-wheeler *Heroine* brought passengers "over the bay" from Mobile to elegant Eastern Shore summer homes and resorts. The famed *Heroine* (pronounced Hero-ine by Fairhope old-timers) was built in Scotland for running the blockade during the Civil War and later used as a Confederate ambulance ship. Around 1890, she was converted into a passenger steamer. (Courtesy Ken Niemeyer.)

The Nelsons and Lowells were early Baldwin County settlers. From left to right, are (seated) Martin Luther and his wife, Ann Nelson Lowell, aunt Blanche, and daughter Pearl; (standing) Martin and Ann's other children—Grover, Hugh, Luther, Orrie, Gordon, Clyde, and Diamond. Many of them became the town's businessmen, bakers, and barbers after Fairhope was founded. (Courtesy Florence Lowell Kellogg.)

Henry George was the influential 19th-century economist whose "single tax" philosophy was the moving spirit behind a group of idealists, many from Iowa, who would settle Fairhope. Their social experiment was based on his theories, inspired by his 1879 book *Progress and Poverty*, which espoused a single tax on land, regardless of improvements.

A group of 28 settlers, including nine children, arrived at Battles Wharf in November 1894 to establish a cooperative colony. The site of the egalitarian town they planned to build on the bay was nearby to the north. Soon after Fairhope was founded, the wharf sported the Battles Pagoda, where visitors could dine and dance on the bay. (Courtesy Palmer Hamilton.)

The colonists bought land that held the cabin and farm of former slaves John Henry Lewis and his wife, Nancy, who figures prominently in the book *Women of Fairhope* by historian Paul M. Gaston. The Lewis family relocated; here one of the Lewis sons, Alfred, his wife, Rosetta Young Lewis, and their children relax on the porch of the later family homestead still standing on Ingleside Avenue. (Courtesy Rosetta Wasp.)

Jerome B. Stapleton was an early Baldwin County settler who, along with his brothers, owned what was called Stapleton's Pasture, where they raised beef cattle on a bluff above Mobile Bay. Their waterfront tract makes up the core of old Fairhope. The single-taxers, who pooled their modest resources, paid $6 an acre for their planned community. (Courtesy Jack Stapleton.)

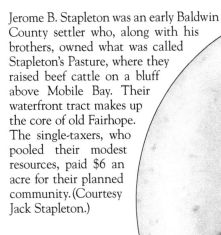

Jerome's wife, Lucy Stapleton, was born in New York State and died in Fairhope at the age of 92. Their property became one of the world's oldest and most successful single-tax colonies and is still owned by the Fairhope Single Tax Corporation, formed by colonists of modest means seeking to establish an ideal society in the late 19th century. (Courtesy Jack Stapleton.)

Only winding wagon lanes, like this one along Fly Creek, crossed the property the settlers chose to start their communal experiment, selecting their site for its beauty and cheap land. Originally called Bayou Volanta by the French, the picturesque creek marked the northern boundary of the town until the 1990s. (Courtesy Rusty Godard.)

Two

A "Fair Hope"

To those who, seeing the vice and misery that spring from the unequal distribution of wealth and privilege, feel the possibility of a higher social state and would strive for its attainment.

—Henry George, *Progress and Poverty*, 1879

The founders named their town Fairhope before it existed because they reckoned it had a "fair hope of success," and they invited a "class of clear-headed and true-hearted reformers" to join their venture to demonstrate Henry George's theories. Here passengers arrive on the steamer *James A. Carney*, which brought the first settlers from Mobile, where they had come by rail with all their possessions. (Courtesy Helen Dyson.)

Ernest Berry Gaston (seated second row center), a young idealist and a founder of the Fairhope Single Tax Corporation (FSTC), brought his wife, Clara Mershon (seated right), mother (seated left), and family from Des Moines, Iowa, to start the experimental colony on Mobile Bay. The children, standing from left to right, are Cornelius, James Ernest, Frances Lilly, Leah Catherine, and Arthur Fairhope "Spider" (seated front center), the first white boy born in Fairhope. (Courtesy FSTC.)

The utopian settlement started with houses for the first five families and a store, with the goal to "establish and maintain a model community or colony free from all forms of private monopoly." Lumber from Mobile was landed on the beach by lighter boat, but by the spring of 1895, the colonists had constructed a wharf. This 1897 view of early Fairhope was taken from Section Street. (Courtesy Harriet Swift.)

20

The Fairhopers' first order of business in their model town was the colony store, the cooperative Fairhope Mercantile, located at the corner of Fairhope Avenue and Section Street, which remains the town's main intersection. The store also served as the post office and central gathering place, especially due to the location of the town well in the foreground. (Courtesy Harriet Swift.)

The same corner 15 years later shows improvements to the main store, now operated by Henry Crawford, and the development along Fairhope Avenue. The colony now boasted its own railroad leading to the wharf at the foot of the street. Engine power would later replace the mule-drawn rail cars in Fairhope, the first and biggest single-tax enclave in the United States. (Courtesy Reed Myers.)

In the early days, everyone kept up with the latest events and announcements by keeping an eye on the local public bulletin board by the newspaper offices downtown. There was a well-attended club meeting or discussion group for civil discourse or heated debate, lecture, or luncheon nearly every day of the week in the town founded by inquiring intellectuals. (Courtesy Reed Myers)

Students at Fairhope's famous Marietta Johnson School of Organic Education pitched in to make wooden street signs for the growing town's main thoroughfares. The private school drew many progressive families to the town. Helen Porter (Dyson), who later taught at the school, is hanging the hand-lettered Fairhope Avenue sign on the post. (Courtesy Helen Dyson.)

The Fairhope House on Magnolia Avenue was the town's first hotel, established in 1897 by single-taxers Delia Knowles Bancroft (left) and husband, George Bancroft (second from left). They met and married in Fairhope. Next to them from left to right are the hotel maid, Elia Lloyd; Delia's orphaned niece, Carrie Betts, who lived with them; and Delia's father, George Knowles, a surveyor and settler from Kansas. (Courtesy Wesley Stapleton.)

George M. Bancroft, who was simply called "The Man" by his family and friends, was an engineer who was active in the FSTC, serving as an early president and helping with its public improvements. Bancroft Street in the uptown commercial district was named in his honor. (Courtesy Wesley Stapleton.)

The Tuvesons, original colonists, enjoy a picnic on the bluff on July 4, 1928. The first Fairhope settlers came from Iowa, Ohio, Minnesota, Pennsylvania, and British Columbia. At first the so-called Yankees populated the Deep South settlement, but area residents began to move to Fairhope after 1899, when the single-taxers allowed others to join their venture. (Courtesy Flora Maye Simmons.)

Adolph Oscar Berglin and his new bride, Eva Bebolt, proudly pose on the day after their December 20, 1900, wedding. A Wisconsin native who became a leading businessman and mayor, Berglin established the Fairhope Ice and Creamery in 1909, one of the first creameries in Alabama. The couple built a large home at the corner of Fairhope Avenue and Church Street. (Courtesy Robert Berglin.)

The family of Clayton Baldwin, who operated a general store, gathers on the front porch of their home, typical of the early modest Fairhope dwellings. The colony advertised that the "vulgar mansions of the predator rich" would not be found there. In the beginning, there was no private ownership of land in Fairhope, where residents had 99-year leases on their FSTC lots. (Courtesy Fairhope Historical Museum.)

By 1913, comfortable Craftsman and Victorian cottages had been built along Fairhope Avenue, the main thoroughfare through what had once been a pine forest. The first three homes on the north side of the first residential block remain, while the fourth, the shotgun Mitchell Cottage, was razed for land speculation in 2004. (Courtesy Reed Myers.)

Homes also rose along the bluff on Bayview Avenue in what founder Gaston once wrote was "a city set upon a hill, shedding its beneficent light to all the world." By 1910, the colony owned over 4,000 acres in the town that was attracting new residents and vacationing visitors. (Courtesy Bill Payne.)

These homes, built on the south side of Magnolia Avenue in the 100 block when the street leading uptown from the bay was dirt, still stand. In the planned community of Fairhope, streets widened as they curved toward the bay to afford everyone a view of the water. Most of these homes were resort guest cottages. (Courtesy Flora Maye Simmons.)

Church Street featured substantial residences, like the two-story house on the far right, which was built by Jonathan Beckner after he moved to Fairhope from Iowa in 1906. Listed on the National Register of Historic Places, it is today the Fairhope Inn and Restaurant at 69 South Church Street. (Courtesy Bill Payne.)

The home of merchant A. P. Minnich, built about 1912, stands at 78 South Section Street. It was once known for the large surrounding orange groves that Minnich planted. Orange and satsuma trees represented a cash crop for many Fairhope residents until a big freeze in 1924 killed the growing citrus industry. (Courtesy Reed Myers.)

Fairhope's site was selected for its natural beauty. Called "Magnolia Cottage, The Home of a Million Roses" on a postcard by photographer Frank Stewart, this attractive home illustrates the fertility of the fragrant garden spot the colonists acquired at the edge of Baldwin County farmland, which remains a breadbasket for the surrounding area. (Courtesy Reed Myers.)

The Fairhope Village Improvement Club (VIC), organized in 1899, sponsored socials and oyster suppers with entertainment to raise funds for public projects. The VIC's first project was a picnic pavilion around the magnolia tree at the beachfront park. Fairhope's far-sighted founders had set aside nearly a mile of beach for public parkland. (Courtesy Claire Totten Gray.)

An early-20th-century bird's-eye view of the intersection of Fairhope Avenue and Section Street shows a prosperous town, with Wheeler's Store, where the Fairhope Esoteric Society held Sunday meetings upstairs, on the left corner. On the right corner is the landmark 1916 Fairhope Pharmacy, the state's oldest in its original location. (Courtesy Pinky Bass.)

By 1912, the colony's cooperative Peoples Railroad had been constructed, with cars carrying goods and passengers from the wharf up Fairhope Avenue and back; however, the rails never ran the 14 miles east to the Louisville and Nashville Railroad at Robertsdale as planned. Soon the horse-and-buggy days would end in Fairhope. (Courtesy Bill Payne.)

Called "a town with a purpose" by the *Fairhope Courier* newspaper, by the early 1920s, the village had many amenities of a larger town, including brick buildings and a theater. This view is looking east up Fairhope Avenue from Church Street. The heart of the experimental colony was becoming a thriving, prosperous urban center. (Courtesy Claire Totten Gray.)

Fairhope incorporated in 1908 with 500 residents and elected its first city council. Seated is the mayor, Dr. Harris S. Greeno, who was not a member of the colony. The councilmen of the new municipality, from left to right, were Nathaniel Mershon, P. Y. Albright, Charles E. Nichols, Clement Coleman, W. Sweet, James Bellangee, and J. M. Pilcher. (Courtesy FSTC.)

An imposing new city hall was built in the popular Spanish Mission Revival style in 1927 by local contractor Oswald Forster, a German native who came to Fairhope in 1912. The landmark at 24 North Section Street also served as the police station and city jail until 2001. This elegant building's original façade remains intact behind a metal false front. (Courtesy Azille Forster Anderson.)

LABOR

"LABOR IS THE BASIS
FOR PRODUCTION
OF ALL WEALTH"

HENRY GEORGE
1839 ——— 1897

THERE SHOULD BE NO
TAXES LEVIED ON MAN'S
PRODUCTIVE ENERGIES

THESE PARKS DONATED BY

SINGLE TAX CORPORATION
SEPTEMBER 29, 1931

A monument at Henry George Park overlooking the bay contains quotes from the social economist whose single-tax philosophy was the guiding spirit behind the colony established on the principle of "cooperative individualism." In the early 1930s, the colony gave the beach and bluff parks and pier to the city for public use. (Courtesy FSTC.)

Three

DREAMERS AND REFORMERS

The "Single Tax" is so simple, so fundamental, and so easy to carry into effect
that I have no doubt that it will be about the last land reform the world will ever get.
People in this world are not often logical.

—Clarence Darrow

The Worcester Single Tax Club, meeting in Massachusetts in the 1890s, probably mirrored the Single Tax Club in Des Moines, Iowa, where the Fairhope experiment began. In 1890, the nation had over 130 single-tax clubs. Prescott A. Parker, seated at center to the left of the man standing, was an engineer and surveyor who settled near Fairhope, where he was an ardent reform proponent. (Courtesy Claude Arnold.)

Ernest Berry Gaston (1861–1938) was Fairhope's foremost founder. The idealistic Populist and Iowa journalist started the influential *Fairhope Courier* newspaper before the town he helped settle in 1894 even existed. A single-taxer influenced by George's philosophy, Gaston was the moving force behind the Fairhope Industrial Association, which became the Fairhope Single Tax Corporation. (Courtesy Rusty Godard.)

Dr. Clara E. Atkinson (1845–1932) was a longtime, well-loved physician in the town where Atkinson Lane is named for her. Pictured here as a young woman before leaving Des Moines, Iowa, she was single-taxer Gaston's half sister. Many independent women were drawn to Fairhope, where they had equal rights and a vote in colony matters. They also held office in the FSTC. (Courtesy Harriet Swift.)

Many adventuresome couples, like this unidentified pair who arrived on August 12, 1904, heartened by Fairhope's promise and reformist zeal, threw their fate to the winds and joined the colony. Though most were poor in pocket, they were rich in spirit. The colony provided newcomers with lots they could rent for 99 years to build homes and plant gardens. (Courtesy Harriet Swift.)

These Fairhopers seem to exhibit a sense of purpose even as they await a bay boat to attend the 1898 Mardi Gras celebration in Mobile, where the first Fat Tuesday observance in the New World took place. While Fairhope was filled with serious-minded reformers, the old French city across the bay let the good times and parades roll during the carnival season. (Courtesy FSTC.)

Alphonso Swift (1838–1915) another settler from Des Moines, arrived on Election Day, November 6, 1896. That was the day Fairhope supporter William Jennings Bryan was defeated for president. Swift owned most of the property in an affluent area that today calls itself the Bluff neighborhood. (Courtesy Harriet Swift.)

Paul Kingston Dealy (1848–1937) brought the Baha'i faith to the South when he moved from Chicago to Fairhope in 1898, attracted by the single-tax theory. Today the religion that believes in one God and one human race has groups in 120,000 localities, including Fairhope. The open-minded town also drew other metaphysical seekers, such as Scientologists and Theosophists. (Courtesy Jim Dealy.)

Clarence Darrow (1857–1938) was the nation's best-known lawyer when he spent his winters in Fairhope lecturing and writing in the 1920s and 1930s. The defender of the underdog had formed the Intercollegiate Socialist Society in Chicago in 1905 with Upton Sinclair, another famous resident. Kathleen Wheeler sculpted Darrow's likeness in Fairhope in 1927. (Courtesy Flora Maye Simmons.)

Coming to Fairhope to recuperate from the famed Scopes monkey trial, Darrow settled his younger sister Ethel in this tiny shotgun cottage (with unidentified family outside) at 83 Magnolia Avenue. The celebrated attorney thought his sister, who had trouble speaking, would be accepted in the small town that had so many eccentrics, and he often visited her here. (Courtesy Pinky Bass.)

Capt. Jack Cross, right, visits with a guest at the Fairhope Hotel he built on Fairhope Avenue at Summit Street after settling in Fairhope in 1908. The English world traveler was called the "Sage of Fairhope." His great friend Darrow called Cross "a very pleasant companion that made me forget my illness and the Fundamentalists and the KKK that surround me." (Courtesy Fairhope Public Library.)

From the beginning, the colony supported education. Organic School teachers Lois Slosson, back left, and Olive Wooster, back right, pose with students c. 1908. From left to right are the following: (first row) Raymond Dyson, Ralph Brown, Grace Coutant, Kirby Wharton, and Rudolph Tuveson; (second row) Eleanor Coutant, Annie Stradling, and three unidentified students; (third row) two unidentified students, Matilda Lilly Bernhardt, Estelle Larson, Frances Kerr Goodrich, ? Coutant, Ester Gilmore, unidentified, Irene Rucker, and Clifford Ernest Johnson. (Courtesy Pinky Bass.)

Henry James Stuart, also called the Hermit and the Old Weaver, moved near Fairhope to die in 1926, but he lived a long philosophical life in a masonry dome hut he built. The fascinating story of Stuart, who rarely wore shoes, inspired the 2005 novel *The Poet of Tolstoy Park* by Fairhope writer and bookman Sonny Brewer. (Courtesy Rusty Godard.)

Progressive educator Marietta Johnson chose Fairhope to open her experimental School of Organic Education in 1907. The school became widely known, as Mrs. Johnson traveled across the United States and Europe lecturing on her educational philosophy and drawing many leaders in their fields of expertise to teach there. Mrs. Johnson is seated on the second row, second from right. (Courtesy Helen Dyson.)

Many Quakers, like Asa Staples from West Branch, Iowa, settled in Fairhope, where the Friends established their own school and meetinghouse. Staples, the town's harness maker, sits in his buggy, with his wife on the porch of their pioneer home, which still stands at 159 Fels Avenue. He would sometimes read papers such as "Philosophy of the Beautiful" at the local Progressive League meetings. (Courtesy Cathy Donelson.)

The House of Totten, on Morphy Avenue, was purchased by Edward P. Totten, a judge and devoted single-taxer, shortly after he came to Fairhope from North Dakota with his young family in 1919. From left to right are Judge Totten and his children: Parker, who was killed in World War II, Claire, and Holly holding baby Joyce. (Courtesy Claire Totten Gray.)

Inquiring minds wanted to know, so Fairhopers turned out for the popular Wednesday Luncheon held in Comings Hall on the Organic School campus. These mid-weekly luncheon gatherings featured discussions, noted speakers, and frequent lectures on topics ranging from philosophy to pure foods. This picture was taken in 1928, when the lunches were 50¢, but they had been a longtime community tradition. (Courtesy Helen Dyson.)

Spiritual matters were also at the heart of the colony's development. The Fairhope Christian Church, where many founding families worshipped, was built in 1901 on a lane that became Church Street. The site of the town's first church is now occupied by the Fairhope Kindergarten Center, which is housed in the first public high school building in the town, built in 1925. (Courtesy Pinky Bass.)

On Easter morning 1915, the Christian church was decorated with flowers and ferns and the choir posed. By 1908, Fairhope had a Baptist church on the next corner, and other denominations soon followed, as people of different creeds and backgrounds came to the cooperative community where all beliefs were respected. (Courtesy Reed Myers.)

Fairhope's first fireplace, the last relic of the original frame Gaston home on Fairhope Avenue, was commemorated by this gathering of the family in later years, when the dream of Fairhope had become a reality. Patriarch E. B. Gaston stands second from left of the old hearth, surrounded by his family members, children, in-laws, and grandchildren. (Courtesy FSTC.)

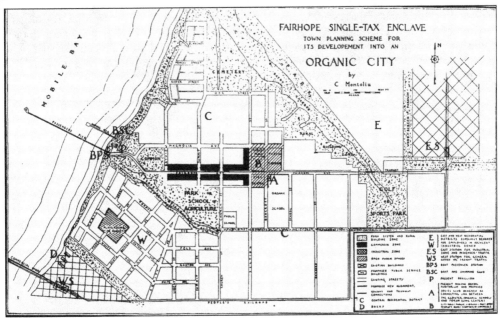

Fairhope was a planned community from the time it was only a concept. In 1922, this organic city plan developed by Cebria de Montoliu, an early proponent of the Utopian Garden City Movement, was supported by the FSTC, but it was never carried out. Montoliu, a Fairhope supporter from Barcelona, Spain, was the secretary of the Hispano-American Garden Cities and Town Planning Association.

Members of the Mobile Business Women's Club relax on the porch of Pine Needles, the elegant retreat they built overlooking the bay in the early 20th century in Fairhope, where women could vote and professional females were treated as equals with their male counterparts. The building at 700 South Mobile Street is today headquarters for American Legion Post 199. (Courtesy Reed Myers.)

Four

SPORTING RESORT

*Moss Bayou is a lovely, easygoing resort town (though not as popular as it once was),
located as it is where Magnolia River runs into the bay with worlds of giant live oaks
and sandy roads that wind forever under the trailing Spanish moss.*

—Robert Bell, *The Butterfly Tree*, 1950

Fairhope author Robert Bell could well have been describing the moss-draped Lover's Lane
south of town when he wrote about the mythical Moss Bayou in his classic novel *The Butterfly
Tree*. In his novel that was really set in Fairhope, Bell wrote of its magic, beauty, and real-life
characters—changing the names, of course. (Courtesy Reed Myers.)

From its beginning, Fairhope was promoted as a seasonal resort and catered to visitors. As early as 1895, the *Fairhope Courier* newspaper reported that the town's location on the Eastern Shore was sought for "excellent bathing, boating and fishing and its health giving breezes from the salt water and piney woods." (Courtesy Rusty Godard.)

A typical scene of visitors flocking to the growing resort town shows members of Woodmen of the World arriving at the wharf in June 1914 from Mobile. Local leaders were promoting tourism, but few roads led into Fairhope at the time, so most of the transportation to the town was still by the bay steamers. (Courtesy Rusty Godard.)

46

"It was a marvelous place that should have been preserved because of its unique personality among elegant hotels in the Deep South," said novelist Robert Bell of the Colonial Inn in a letter reproduced in the 2001 book *Meet Me at the Butterfly Tree* by Fairhope writer Mary Lois Timbes. The inn was once the town's grandest resort. (Courtesy Claire Gray.)

There was always a party going on somewhere in Fairhope, which had a population laced with fun-loving visitors and charming eccentrics. Here a group pretending to be pirates poses together to commemorate their costume party held at the Colonial Inn. (Courtesy Ken Niemeyer.)

Team sports were encouraged by Lydia Newcomb Comings, a nationally recognized writer and lecturer on physical education who co-founded the Organic School in Fairhope. Here students do exercises in the schoolyard, while others play tennis on a clay court. Community tennis courts were also located on the bay bluff. (Courtesy Helen Dyson.)

An old-fashioned game of croquet is played about 1910 on the grounds of a family home called the Columns. Edwin Clayton and Cornelia Slosson moved to Fairhope from nearby Silverhill about 1908 and bought the neoclassical revival house on the northeast corner of Magnolia and Bayview Avenues. (Courtesy Pinky Bass.)

Basketball was still in its infancy in 1918—the indoor game was invented in 1891 to bridge the season between football and baseball—but Fairhope had a team. Members of the Fairhope Athletic Club's 1918 team were identified as, from left to right, (standing) Martin, Stapleton, Galbraith, Titus, and Stimpson; (seated) Souter, Johnson, and Mershon. (Courtesy Rusty Godard.)

The Fairhope Athletic Club football team poses on the steps of the Bell Building at the Organic School, looking like the members are ready to take on all comers in 1921. That was the year the National Football League was organized. The sport was and still is popular in Fairhope. (Courtesy Helen Dyson.)

Daredevils wait their turn for a spine-tingling ride down the giant water slide named the Thriller at the Fairhope pier c. 1913. The slide was a leading attraction on Mobile Bay in its time, drawing tourists for thrills and possibly spills into the warm waters of the bay. (Courtesy Pinky Bass.)

Ellen Slosson (far left), blind since childhood, braves the slide with, from left to right, her sister's children Ruth, Marion, Frances, and Edward. The children's mother, Lois Sundberg, was an early woman photographer who captured her family's activities and many other Fairhope scenes, providing the community with a valuable historic photographic record. (Courtesy Pinky Bass.)

The Magnolia Beach Pavilion was a popular waterfront spot, as was the old casino at the Fairhope pier in the distance. The casino was a bathhouse and social hall and not a gambling establishment; however, many visitors and Fairhope residents back in the Roaring Twenties were not averse to a friendly wager over a game of cards. (Courtesy Reed Myers.)

Tourists head back to the bay boats after enjoying a summer day in Fairhope. The town drew several thousand visitors on holidays, and the casino in the background was the town's biggest entertainment spot. Without large industry, a big part of Fairhope's economy was based on spending by visitors, as is the case today. (Courtesy Fairhope Historical Museum.)

Hunting was a sport as well as a means of putting food on the table in the early days, when Fairhope was surrounded by woods. Curtis Rockwell (far left), who shot the deer, holds the wagon team that he brought from Iowa when he settled his Quaker family in Fairhope in 1915. (Courtesy Marietta Johnson Museum.)

From left to right, Ernest Swift and friends Frank and Bill Davis head out to the fields for a hunt with their rifles and dogs in the early 20th century. A ladder to a tree-fork deer stand is in the background. Swift came to Fairhope as a boy in 1896 and became the longtime town policeman, nicknamed "Swifty." (Courtesy Harriet Swift.)

These hunters bagged an alligator. Standing from left to right are Sim Andrews, Ralph "Cotton" Brown, Rudolph "Reckless" Tuveson, and Harris "Quaker" Rockwell. Bill Schuler is at the head and Ed Wood at the tail. The Gulf and bay were a fishing paradise, drawing sportsmen from over the country, and fish camps still abound in the area. (Courtesy Flora Maye Simmons.)

In the foreground from left to right, the Sundberg siblings, Ruth, Edwin, Frances, and Marion, catch a mess of blue crabs at the Fairhope pier, still a prime spot for crabbing, fishing, and experiencing glorious sunny days. Behind the children, family friend Mrs. McLaughlin pauses to adjust her sun hat. (Courtesy Pinky Bass.)

The Fairhope Golf, Gun, and Country Club opened in 1916 with a nine-hole course designed by famed golf architect Walter Fovargue of Chicago. The golf course on Fairhope Avenue east of Marshall's Gully was subdivided into residential lots in the 1950s, but its clubhouse still stands at 651 Johnson Avenue. (Courtesy Harriet Swift.)

Mr. and Mrs. George Yonk Skinner (the couple at far left) join a fashionable golfing party in front of the clubhouse, now a residence. The Craftsman-style clubhouse, which also hosted parties and dances, was built on FSTC land to attract winter visitors from the North. It was dedicated at a New Year's Night celebration in 1923. (Courtesy Ken Niemeyer.)

Sailors lounge on the porch of the Eastern Shore Yacht Club. It was built after a 1916 hurricane destroyed the Mobile Yacht Club, the oldest on the Gulf Coast. In the 1940s, the building on South Mobile Street became the La Corona dance club, open to teenagers until 9 p.m. and adults only the rest of the evening. (Courtesy Flora Maye Simmons.)

These graceful fish boats racing on the bay's premier sailing waters originated in 1918. The new fish class inspired the formation of the five-state Gulf Yachting Association (GYA). Fairhope's first yacht club was an original member of the GYA, which began the famed Lipton Cup Regatta. The present Fairhope Yacht Club on Bayou Volanta was founded in 1942. (Courtesy Cathy Donelson.)

Picnicking under the fragrant pines in the gentle breezes on the bay bluff has always been part of the laid-back lifestyle in Fairhope, where outdoor community gatherings are a tradition. Here a group gathers at a long table decked with linens, china, and, no doubt, homemade delicacies and Fairhope's famous seafood. (Courtesy Robert Berglin.)

Fairhope's balmy weather and slow pace engrossed others in more sedate outdoor activities such as reading on the peaceful bluff promenade. Naturalist William Bartram passed through the area in the late 18th century, and his blissful descriptions of its magnificent magnolia groves and scenery in his book *Travels* influenced romantic poet Samuel Coleridge's imagery in *Kubla Khan*.

Five

AN ART COLONY

*My cabin was on a strip of beach and beyond the beach the mouth of a river
came down into the bay. Banking the two shores of the river were wharfs
where boats came in and tied up to receive cargo and from where boats went out
to the ports of the world.*

—Sherwood Anderson, *Paris Notebook*, 1921

Sherwood Anderson, acclaimed for *Winesburg, Ohio*, which made him a force in the American short story, retreated to Fairhope in 1920. He wrote in a cabin in the woods, perhaps someplace like this typical rustic waterfront cottage near town. His wife, Tennessee Mitchell, used local models to create clay faces to illustrate his story collection *The Triumph of the Egg*. (Courtesy Rusty Godard.)

Marie Howland was a Socialist writer and free-love advocate who came to Fairhope in 1899 from an intentional community at Topolobampo, Mexico, shown here. Author of the famous labor novel *The Familistre,* she became associate editor of the *Fairhope Courier* and helped establish the town's library with her extensive rare-book collection. (Courtesy Topolobampo Collections, Special Collections, California State University, Fresno.)

The highly literate residents of Fairhope heavily patronized the original small public library. The building at 10 North Summit Street served from 1906 to 1983 and is now a part of the headquarters of the University of South Alabama Baldwin County campus. When Mrs. Howland died in 1921, a service was held in the library she founded. (Courtesy Cathy Donelson.)

Frank Stewart (1855–1942) was "The Picture Man," who preserved a priceless record of Fairhope in his photographs documenting the town and its people from the beginning. Stewart, perhaps the area's most important artist and visual historian, is shown here washing prints in a clear stream. No photographic book about Fairhope would be complete without his superb and valuable legacy of silvered prints. (Courtesy Pinky Bass.)

Upton Sinclair possibly attended friend Anna Pope Randolph's wedding on the bay front. America's most famous writer when he spent part of 1909 and 1910 in Fairhope, he wrote his novel *Love's Pilgrimage* in a tent on the bay bluff. Celebrated for his muckraking book *The Jungle*, Sinclair believed in single-tax communal living and wrote about Fairhope in his essay "Enclaves of Economic Rent." (Courtesy Pinky Bass.)

Olive "Piney" Wood Gaston was a well-respected Fairhope musician and published poet. She played the piano for decades at weddings, churches, and Organic School folk dances. Arriving from McGregor, Iowa, in 1911 with her widowed mother, she later married the first man she saw when she stepped off the bay boat: James E. Gaston. (Courtesy Barry Gaston.)

Lydia J. Newcomb Comings was another of the town's remarkable women. The noted physical education teacher, writer, and lecturer had studied and traveled throughout Europe. The pioneer who helped found the Organic School also served as president of the FSTC. She also was prominent in club and library work and was a historian who founded the Baldwin County Historical Society. (Courtesy Helen Dyson.)

The Magnet Theater, built in 1924, was the longest-running movie house in South Alabama when it closed in the mid-1970s. Built of local Clay City tile by attorney and entrepreneur Edward P. Totten, it also featured a tearoom called the Tea Tile. The landmark at the corner of Fairhope Avenue and Church Street has been converted into shops, but the original projection booth remains upstairs. (Courtesy Claire Totten Gray.)

The sumptuous interior of the Magnet, designed by Mobile architect J. Platt Roberts, was remarkable for a small South Alabama town like Fairhope, where fewer than 1,000 souls lived. The cinema also drew crowds from the countryside. The theater's builder, Judge Edward P. Totten, was fascinated about the future of moving pictures and had first started showing movies at the Organic School. (Courtesy Claire Totten Gray.)

The colony filled with artists, writers, and musicians even has its own song, titled "Fairhope," with lyrics by early councilman J. M. Pilcher and music by his wife, Hazel, a graduate of the Boston Musical Conservatory. Here the Baldwin County Orchestra, made up of mostly Fairhope musicians, poses with their instruments in the 1920s in front of the old public school building. (Courtesy FSTC.)

Architecture also was art in the distinctive settlement that featured many one-of-a-kind structures. Emma Schramm, a self-sufficient teacher, started building her home out of trees and mud and cement about 1915. Trycadia Lodge, now demolished, illustrates the individualist character and grit of many who were drawn to Fairhope. (Courtesy Claire Totten Gray.)

The Greeno Masonic Lodge, with downstairs post office, was one of Fairhope's first two-story masonry buildings. The structure at 66 South Section Street, built in 1911 by English-born local builder Marmaduke Dyson, featured a molded masonry block made of indigenous materials such as beach sand. The dimpled Dyson concrete would become a distinctive early building block of Fairhope. (Courtesy Pinky Bass.)

Fairhope's next post office, designed and built by prominent contractor Dyson and his sons in 1932, is listed on the National Register as the county's finest Italian Renaissance Revival architecture. It now houses the historic *Fairhope Courier* newspaper at 325 Fairhope Avenue. To the right, the Dyson-built Bloxom Building is another registered landmark important for its art-deco style. (Courtesy Palmer Hamilton.)

The Mecca, a whimsical service station built by Gulf Oil dealer and contractor Oswalt Forster about 1936, featured a pergola-style roof topped by a lighthouse cupola. The old gas station at 218 Fairhope Avenue is one of several in town that have been recycled into boutique shops catering to the tourist trade. (Courtesy Azille Forster Anderson.)

The First Church of Christ, Scientist, at 301 Fels Avenue, another Forster building, looks like a miniature Greek temple with its distinctive Tuscan columns. Built in the late 1930s, the Christian Scientist church graces a residential street named for Fairhope benefactor Joseph Fels of Philadelphia, a wealthy single-taxer and philanthropist who made his fortune with Fels Naphtha Soap. (Courtesy Azille Forster Anderson.)

Robert Bell captured Fairhope's enchantment in his coming-of-age novel *The Butterfly Tree,* published in 1959. In a search of the mystical butterfly tree, he portrays a dream world called Moss Bayou but bases characters on real people. "Miss Claverly" was Winifred Duncan, another Fairhope writer, dancer, and eccentric naturalist who wrote *The Private Life of the Protozoa.* (Courtesy Bill Bell.)

Bell called Gretchen Riggs his guru. An important part of Fairhope's artistic community, she had studied abroad and also at the American Academy of Dramatic Art. As a musician, Broadway stage actress, teacher, mystic, and self-described psychic, she was a mentor to youngsters and a moving force behind many plays at the local Theatre 98. (Courtesy Stephen Riggs.)

Music and art were an important part of life in Fairhope, where the students at the School of Organic Education had their own band. The school's original Bell Building at 10 South School Street now houses the Marietta Johnson Museum. The Fairhope Historical Museum is in another wing. The town also features the Eastern Shore Art Center and numerous private galleries. (Courtesy Marietta Johnson Museum.)

Dr. John Dewey was one of the nation's many influential thinkers and writers who made pilgrimages to Fairhope. Some who settled in the art colony included noted children's book author and illustrator Anna Braune, philosopher Baker Brownell, and prolific authors Frances Gaither and Eleanor Risley. (Courtesy University of Chicago, Center for Dewey Studies.)

Six

EXTRAORDINARY
EDUCATION

Mrs. Johnson is trying an experiment under conditions which hold in public schools, and she believes that her methods are feasible for any public school system. She charges practically no tuition, and any child is welcome. She calls her methods of education "organic" because they follow the natural growth of the pupil.

—John Dewey, *Schools of To-Morrow*, 1914

The frontispiece of John Dewey's influential book *Schools of To-Morrow* features Marietta Johnson teaching outside at her famous School of Organic Education. The scene is also the model for the bronze sculpture grouping on the Fairhope bluff. Dewey, the past century's foremost educator and philosopher, centered his groundbreaking book on education around Mrs. Johnson's school after visiting in 1913.

Marietta Johnson (1864–1938), known around the world as a progressive educator, opened her experimental school in the colony in 1907, drawing intellectuals from all over the country to teach there. A founder of the Progressive Education Association who lectured across America and Europe, she authored two books, *Youth in a World of Men* and *Thirty Years with an Idea*. (Courtesy Marietta Johnson Museum.)

Teachers' training classes were often conducted outdoors on the Fairhope campus. Dewey wrote, "To this spot during the past few years students and experts have made pilgrimages, and the influence of Mrs. Johnson's model has led to the starting of similar schools in different parts of the United States." (Courtesy Marietta Johnson Museum.)

Children do handwork in a class outside *c.* 1910. "Nature has not adapted the young animal to the narrow desk, the crowded curriculum, the silent absorption of complicated facts," Dewey wrote about Mrs. Johnson's practice of holding classes out of doors. Early-20th-century progressives such as Upton Sinclair and poet Vachel Lindsay sent their children to the Organic School. (Courtesy Pinky Bass.)

The Organic School began in the Bell Building, a former public school building, and the FSTC provided a 10-acre campus in 1909. Here students join teachers in roofing the new Domestic Science building, where children helped prepare hot 10¢ lunches for students. Clarence Darrow also lectured at the school on subjects such as Tolstoy to help raise funds. (Courtesy Helen Dyson.)

Students learned by doing at the Organic School and studied American Indian history and culture by creating teepee villages. Mrs. Johnson believed that children should learn to work together and have healthy activity. She discouraged teaching them to read at an early age. Life classes at the school were made up of general age groupings, with the youngest ones in First Life. (Courtesy Claire Gray.)

The gullies near the school were an exciting place to explore and also served as outdoor textbooks for nature study and geology lessons illustrating soil and rock formation. Archery classes also were held in the deep ravines. In 1908, a school group gathers in a gully for lessons with teachers and Mrs. Johnson, who is at the far left. (Courtesy Robert Berglin.)

70

This overview of campus shows the growth of the Organic School in the 1920s, at its peak. In the late 1980s, the school sold its campus, which now holds Faulkner State Community College. The original Bell Building has been restored and is a museum. The school, entering its second century, continues to operate on a smaller scale in a new facility in Fairhope. (Courtesy Reed Myers.)

The gullies running through Fairhope down to Mobile Bay served as walkways through the town for many years. Here another group of Organic School students pauses during a field trip to pose in one of the gullies, where the walls were often used as chalkboards. Classes were held outside whenever possible, weather permitting. (Courtesy Robert Berglin.)

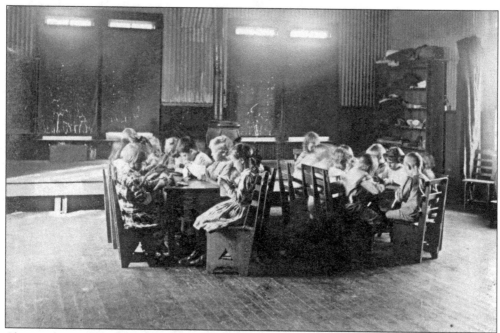

Classes also were held inside at the Organic School. In the early days, the school held no examinations and no homework was assigned, so children would have more time for play. The philosophy at the nationally known experimental school was that no child should be allowed to fail. (Courtesy Pinky Bass.)

May Day, with the maypole dance, was one of the many festivals celebrated at the progressive school, where play was emphasized as an important part of learning. Non-competitive and creative games were encouraged. "The greatest minds," Mrs. Johnson wrote, "are those able to use the play spirit in work." (Courtesy Helen Dyson.)

72

Everyone was welcome to join in the folk dancing at the school, evidenced by this robust scene in front of the Bell Building. Dance was one of the required subjects for both boys and girls at the Organic School, and many community dances were held on the campus in the heart of town over the years. (Courtesy Marietta Johnson Museum.)

Students demonstrate folk dance on the green at the Old Globe Theater in San Diego in the 1930s. Organic School dancers performed across the country, from California to Chicago to Washington, D.C. Mrs. Johnson, who believed folk dancing was adapted to the schoolroom, wrote, "It is objective and purposeful, it is highly social and very beautiful." (Courtesy Claire Gray.)

The male students at the Organic School kept alive the tradition of the ancient Morris Dance, an old ritual English dance, along with the sword dance and other folk dances. Charles Rabold, a protégé of the leading English folklorist, Cecil Sharp, left Yale University to teach at the school, turning the Fairhope dance program into one of the best in the country. (Courtesy Marietta Johnson Museum.)

Even the little ones, dressed here in fairy costumes, learned the dances. Storytelling and dramatization often took the place of bookwork at the school. Students made their own costumes and acted out myths and stories. Often they would perform an entire literary tale without direction from a teacher. (Courtesy Marietta Johnson Museum.)

"Uncle Sam," at right, is part of a patriotic program at the Organic School. Renowned anthropologist Margaret Mead's younger sisters attended the Fairhope school. Mead later wrote that Elizabeth graduated, but her sister Priscilla insisted "I am not organic" and opted for a more traditional education back East. (Courtesy Marietta Johnson Museum.)

Boats made at the school were launched in the bay in the early 1920s. Both boys and girls took shop at the school, which drew master craftsmen as teachers. Wharton Esherick, who became a nationally known woodcutter and artist called the "Dean of the American Craftsmen," taught students math in 1919 by making woodworking measurements. (Courtesy Marietta Johnson Museum.)

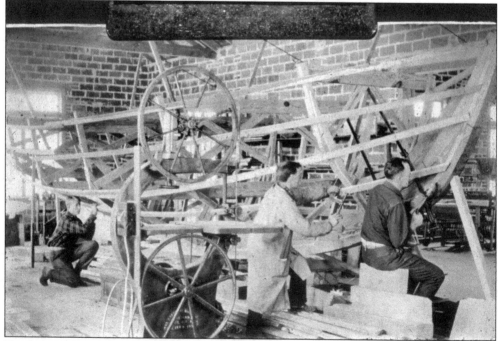

Teachers work on the *Osprey* sailboat in the Manual Arts Building at the Organic School as part of shop class. The wooden boat sailed the waters of the Gulf for several decades. Students also made tables and chairs for the school classrooms in the shop building. (Courtesy Marietta Johnson Museum.)

The annual Silver Tea was a tradition at the school, where students raised funds by selling their exquisite hand-made silver jewelry and artwork. Master silversmiths, weavers, potters, and sculptors on the school faculty taught the crafts. This Silver Tea was held at the school in the 1940s. (Courtesy Marietta Johnson Museum.)

The Friends School, left, was started in 1915 for children of Quaker families who came to Fairhope. The Meeting House was built next door for worship in 1919, but before that, the meetings were held in the schoolhouse. Remodeled into business use, the school still stands by the Friends Meeting House east of town on Fairhope Avenue. (Courtesy Cecil Rockwell.)

Pageants also were part of the educational program at Fairhope's public school, where students celebrated Thanksgiving with this program in 1914. The town had a public educational system from its earliest days. The first school was in a small frame building uptown in Fairhope, where schooling was mandatory, according to the colony's original constitution. (Courtesy Robert Berglin.)

Everyone walked to school when Fairhope was a village. In 1909, this new public school was built at the corner of Church and Morphy. The large building, demolished in 1979, housed all grades until 1925, when a new high school was built across the street. The Fairhoper's Community Park, built by volunteers, is on the site of the former school. (Courtesy Reed Myers.)

Seven

ON THE MOVE

*Rowing is a sport for dreamers. As long as you put in the work, you can own the dream.
When the work stops, the dream disappears.*

—Haywood Broun

Sportswriter Haywood Broun, who attended school in Fairhope, was the son of noted Haywood Hale Broun, member of the famed Algonquin Circle. He may have been remembering idyllic days rowing on the bay, like these youngsters. Here contractor Reuben E. Sundberg plays with his four children in a boat flying an American flag. (Courtesy Pinky Bass.)

The *Nettie Quill*, loaded with goods and passengers, made trips from Mobile up the Alabama River and back and brought many Fairhope settlers downriver. Fairhope author Eleanor de la Vergne Risley, who wrote about pioneer life in Alabama, described the riverboat in *The Road to Wildcat*, published in 1930. (Courtesy Rusty Godard.)

The first order of business in the fledgling settlement was a wharf and steamer to bring supplies over from the port of Mobile and move residents back and forth across the bay, so the colony built its own boat, *Fairhope*, in 1900. Fares on the bay boat with the distinctive red smokestack were 25¢. (Courtesy FSTC.)

Herman Mannich, shown here in 1915, operated the Mannich Ferry across Fish River at Marlow. As a boy, the pioneer witnessed Adm. David G. Farragut's fleet in the river after the Civil War battle of Mobile Bay in 1864. Mannich Ferry was on an early trail from Pensacola, one of the few overland routes to Fairhope, as most transportation was by water. (Courtesy Bobby Mannich.)

One of the first industrial ventures was a sawmill to provide lumber for building. Oxen hauled heavy pine logs from the woods and also pulled the milled timbers and boards. Townspeople claimed they could recognize an ox driver by the rolling gait he developed from walking beside his team—even if he was dressed for church. (Courtesy Helen Dyson.)

Cows also pulled their loads in Fairhope. Here some children ride on a cow wagon along Church Street. In the background is the home of the Browns, who owned a sawmill and brickyard where Thomas Hospital is today. The house is now a coffee shop at 302 Delamare Avenue. (Courtesy Robert Berglin.)

"Native Automobull" is the tongue-in-cheek title early-20th-century photographer Frank Stewart gave this picture he took of a woman and boy with a steer-drawn cart. Wagons and carts were the main mode of transportation through the piney-wood lanes around Fairhope for those who did not have automobiles. (Courtesy Reed Myers.)

The postal carrier pauses to pose for the camera while driving the small U.S. Mail buggy through Fairhope. Onlookers seem to await delivery of mail, which came over the bay daily from Mobile on the mail packet *Lucille*. Letters were often addressed with the name of a residence, because Fairhopers were fond of naming their cottages. (Courtesy Marietta Johnson Museum.)

Alf Kyle, who was the director of the reptile section of the Bronx Zoo in New York, takes a break from snake hunting by hitching a playful ride down Section Street. In Fairhope to visit relatives, Kyle also spent time collecting specimens for the zoo, and there's no doubt he found many. (Courtesy Claire Gray.)

The Berglin and McBroom parents watch from the porch of the Pinequat Shop as their children go for a ride down Fairhope Avenue in 1914 in a double-seated miniature wagon pulled by a large sheep. The Berglins' home, which no longer stands, was moved from Fairhope Avenue around the corner to Church Street to make way for construction of the Magnet Theater. (Courtesy Robert Berglin.)

Children used to catch rides on the horse-drawn milk wagon as it made its rounds of the town. Soon horse and mule-powered vehicles would be replaced, as new motorized modes of transportation made their way to Fairhope, which was still a small island-like enclave. (Courtesy Harriet Swift.)

Buggies ran alongside the rails in 1912 when track for the Peoples Railroad, a company sponsored by the colony, began to be laid along Fairhope Avenue to the wharf. Here ties are stacked for the train line that was planned to connect the town to the nation's railway system, but it never grew beyond local service. (Courtesy Robert Berglin.)

The first railroad cars were pulled by mules, but by 1920, motorcars with Ford engines pulled the loads up to 15,000 pounds to help with the shipment of outgoing crates of locally grown oranges and other goods. Here passengers ride uptown on the rails that were the small town's economic lifeline. (Courtesy Reed Myers.)

From left to right, the Swift children, Susan, Jane, and Philip, show off different types of kiddy vehicles, including a tiny wagon and early tricycle. They also rode a small donkey about town in the days before parents had to be concerned about traffic and children playing in the streets in Fairhope. (Courtesy Harriet Swift.)

Motorized vehicles became available after the turn of the century, beginning with the popularity of Henry Ford's affordable automobiles. Here a procession of cars turns the steep curve off Fairhope Avenue onto Mobile Street, towing a newly constructed boat to the launch. Knoll Park is in the background. (Courtesy Harriet Swift.)

Edwin Clayton Slosson, left, and brother Gene ride in *Sarah Jane* in 1911. Slosson, a New York native, owned a sawmill and machine shop. Once they were not able to stop the car, so they circled the yard and finally lassoed a tree. The Holsman auto, which was guided by a lever, previously belonged to Dr. C. L. Mershon. (Courtesy Pinky Bass.)

Flight also came to Fairhope. Walter Forster built this one-passenger glider out of Honduran mahogany and pulled it over the water with a speedboat he named the *Azille* after his daughter. The Forster brothers gathered by the plane are Herbert (left), Fred (right), and Walter (kneeling). (Courtesy Azille Forster Anderson.)

The town turned out for the visit of the Twenty Millionth Ford. This 1931 Model A touring the country for publicity was once displayed in the Henry Ford Museum. James Gaston, who had started with an auto livery business in 1914, later opened an early Ford dealership in this c. 1920 building, still standing at 403 Fairhope Avenue. (Courtesy Helen Porter Dyson.)

Eight

BUSINESS IS BOOMING

Let us show that from under the mild skies of Alabama shall come forth another colony,
a little economic child of social justice that shall lead the misdirected,
but terribly destructive forces of modern society to lie down together.

—E. B. Gaston

Called a poor man's effort by newspaper publisher E. B. Gaston, Fairhope grew from a concept to a community. At the far right is the original office of the *Fairhope Courier*. First published in Des Moines, Iowa, in the fall of 1894, before settlers left for Alabama, it reported "Fairhope's Model Community will be a reality within a few weeks." (Courtesy Harriet Swift.)

The Pinequat Shop, built in 1899, was the town's oldest operating business until 1959, when it was demolished to make way for a new bank building at 387 Fairhope Avenue. The shop specialized in local souvenirs like chinaberry beads, candied figs, and kumquat jellies, in addition to fancy ladies' hats. (Courtesy Rusty Godard.)

Fairhope's economy centered on tourism and catering to visitors. The casino, which dominated the bay beach by the pier, was the local bathhouse and gathering place for swimming and entertainment. The summer season was a busy one, with many groups making day trips from Mobile on the bay steamers. (Courtesy Reed Myers.)

Other places such as Whittier Hall, which opened in 1911, catered only to winter visitors. The showplace hotel at 201 Magnolia Avenue, now a residence, was operated by Mr. and Mrs. A. N. Whittier. They had been in the florist business in Niagara Falls and planted semi-tropical plants on the hotel grounds. (Courtesy Reed Myers.)

The Colonial Inn stood on Mobile Street overlooking the bay. Here an interesting group is gathered on the grounds of the hotel that attracted well-heeled sophisticates from the East and cities like Chicago. Many Northerners came to Fairhope to spend the winter months, enjoying the mild climate away from the ice and snow. (Courtesy Ken Niemeyer.)

This early turpentine still on the bay was part of an important local industry that provided a livelihood for many men in the community. They gathered the sap from the plentiful pine trees in the area for the turpentine-making operations. The industry had existed long before Fairhope was founded. (Courtesy Harriet Swift.)

Every town had a blacksmith shop, but King Vanderslice's shop went up in flames in 1916. Townspeople fought to keep the fire from spreading to the garage next door, where gasoline drums were stored. Curious children inspect the charred remains from the blaze that destroyed Vanderslice's automobile as well as the motorcycle of his helper, Rudolph Tuveson. (Courtesy Reed Myers.)

A. O. Berglin's ice plant on the bay was one of the early industries in Fairhope, which boasted a population of nearly 500 by 1904. The business later expanded into a creamery, which became famous for its delicious Azalea brand ice cream. Mr. Berglin stands at the right, while his wife, Eva, and children pose in the surrey. (Courtesy Reed Myers.)

Tobacco grew in nearby Robertsdale and the surrounding area. In 1894—the colony's first year—a cigar factory shipped 800 "Fairhope" cigars to Chicago and Mobile for sale. The economic venture was short-lived, possibly because the local product was not that good 5¢ cigar everyone was hoping to find. (Courtesy Pinky Bass.)

This view looking west toward the bay on Fairhope Avenue at Section Street shows the main mercantile corner about 1914 with the town water tank that replaced the well. By this time, Fairhope had its own electricity plant and home-owned telephone company in addition to a public waterworks and railroad venture. (Courtesy FSTC.)

This handsome new brick Peoples Cooperative Store, completed in 1922, embodied Fairhope's ideals and carried everything from shoes to plowshares. Community meetings and Thursday afternoon forums were held in the spacious upstairs auditorium. The corner building at 310 Fairhope Avenue is still a hardware store. To its right was the town's furniture store, now a downtown restaurant building. (Courtesy Reed Myers.)

94

The Bank of Fairhope (right) at the corner of Section Street and Johnson Avenue was the town's first bank in 1917. It was the only county bank to weather the Great Depression, and the building now serves another business use. At left was the original 1924 Fairhope Coal and Supply at 31 Section Street. Later incorporated into a grocery market, it is now a dress shop. (Courtesy Fairhope Historical Museum.)

The Fairhope Hatchery occupied the Coal and Supply building from about 1929 to 1943. Operated by a prominent Quaker family, it hatched about 5,000 chicks a week. To the right is owner and early Fairhope settler Arthur Rockwell, and at left is his son and business partner Cecil. (Courtesy Cecil Rockwell.)

The post office and Greeno Masonic Lodge (far left) dominated Section Street, seen here looking north. The lodge at 66 South Section Street, built in 1911, was named in honor of Fairhope's first mayor, Dr. Harris S. Greeno, who donated the land for the building. Up the way was the Knights of Pythias Lodge. (Courtesy Fairhope Historical Museum.)

The Fairhope Garage at 25 South Section Street was built in 1924 and originally was a paint store. The building, with its distinctive contoured parapet, was built on the site of Fairhope's first school, which was in a small frame building. The building has served several commercial uses over its life, also housing a laundry and gift shop. (Courtesy Flora Maye Simmons.)

Called the "Pythian Castle" when dedicated in 1915, the former Knights of Pythias Fairhope Lodge still stands at 52 South Section Street, though heavily remodeled for business use since the lodge disbanded in the 1940s. The upstairs of the building, one of the few Pythian lodges in South Alabama, was also used for Fairhope Forum and Theosophical Society meetings. (Courtesy Rusty Godard.)

Arthur Mannich, center, stands in the early 1940s front of his Mannich's City Market and Grocery, which operated until about 1974 in downtown Fairhope. The building at 31 South Section Street has since housed several other businesses. Now the Colony Shop is located on the north side. (Courtesy Bob Mannich.)

97

By the 1920s, Fairhope Avenue had everything but a jail. "No resident of Fairhope has been a defendant in a criminal case in county court. Perhaps I should add that there is no place except the county court where anyone could be a defendant; there has never been a court or jail or anything of that sort in Fairhope," wrote Upton Sinclair in "Enclaves of Economic Rent" in 1924.

Ed Niemeyer tends the soda fountain in the late 1930s at Brad's, operated by his brother Brad. The popular eatery in the 1928 Walker Building at 384 Fairhope Avenue later became the Soda Garden. Shell's Five and Dime was next door. Today the restored building holds ground-floor specialty shops with business offices upstairs. (Courtesy Ken Niemeyer.)

Norvin DuBrock and his wife, Sybilla, await customers at their laundry counter. DuBrock's Laundry operated for many years in the 1928 building at 7–11 North Church Street. The masonry building still features the remains of a brick furnace that helped fire the boilers for the steam-driven laundry equipment, which worked on a system of pulleys. (Courtesy George DuBrock.)

The *Fairhope Courier* staff works in the old newspaper make-up room at 336 Fairhope Avenue. They are, from left to right, Arthur Fairhope "Spider" Gaston; Henry Crawford; Henry's mother, editor Frances "Frankie" Gaston Crawford; and Ned Doughtery. The Gaston family published the influential newspaper from 1894, starting it in Iowa, until it was sold in 1964. (Courtesy Rusty Godard.)

The town turned out for the opening of Greer's supermarket in the late 1940s at its new location on South Section Street. The original grocery first opened a block away about 1928 at 24 South Section Street, at the corner of Delamare Avenue. It was the first chain store in Fairhope, where the entire downtown business district has been nominated to the National Register of Historic Places.

Nine

CELEBRATION
AND DRAMA

We lived our little drama
We kissed in a field of white
And stars fell on Alabama last night

—"Stars Fell on Alabama," Mitchell Parish and Frank S. Perkins, 1934

A group of young wags formed a semi-secret society called the Paw Paw Keewans and built their log clubhouse on a lane called Pig Alley. Calling themselves the PPKs, whose real meaning still remains a mystery, they enjoyed poking fun at the serious side of Fairhope, where many older residents attended meetings of organizations like the Henry George Club. (Courtesy Harriet Swift.)

The completed PPK Club on Pig Alley, later renamed Delamare Avenue and now an upscale shopping district with antique and gift shops and art galleries, became a social center. The log cabin was the scene of dances, theatrical performances, and shows, such as a satire titled "Old Fairhope" presented by the PPK Minstrels. (Courtesy Flora Maye Simmons.)

In 1916, the PPK Minstrels presented a locally written and produced show titled "Humble Yo'sef Brother, Humble Yo'sef." The back of this postcard said that some of the performers were from Hyde Park, Chicago, showing that seasonal visitors from out of town also participated in Fairhope productions. (Courtesy Reed Myers.)

"Thanksgiving in Fairhope" is the title of this 1924 photograph of hunters returning from the turkey woods in nearby Spanish Fort with gobblers for the holiday tables. The three hunters displaying their game are, from left to right, Norris Stapleton, Harve Wilson, and Warren Stearns. (Courtesy Harmon Stearns.)

Civil War veterans arrived in Fairhope in January 1913 for the annual old soldiers reunion held in the town. Founded by people from different areas of the country, Fairhope was exceptional among small Southern towns in that it had more Union veterans than those who served on the Confederate side. (Courtesy FSTC.)

From the beginning, Independence Day called for picnics and a special community observance on the bay front. Here a group gathered on the steps, which still exist at the bluff park on South Mobile Street, to wave their flags for a Fourth of July celebration in the early 20th century. (Courtesy Pinky Bass.)

The 1906 Fourth of July celebration featured fireworks and a Buffalo Bill cowboy and Indians show sponsored by the firemen to attract visitors downtown. Hundreds of visitors used to come across the bay for Fairhope's doings on the Fourth, and today thousands come to watch the annual fireworks extravaganza produced by the Fairhope Volunteer Fire Department. (Courtesy FSTC.)

Several elaborate parades with floats move down Fairhope's streets during the Mardi Gras season. These costumed children in masks and crowns celebrated Fat Tuesday in 1908 by riding in carts. Fairhope's new arrivals were quick to take up the old Gulf Coast observation of Mardi Gras, which originated in Mobile, not New Orleans, which was founded later by the French. (Courtesy Robert Berglin.)

Fairhope was the kind of place where people got together to make elaborate and artistic floats and decorations for any occasion. Here a group of local residents participate in the Festival of Nations at nearby Battles Wharf in August 1909. Different floats were designed to honor the heritage of area settlers from other countries. (Courtesy Pinky Bass.)

Fairhope mayor William McIntosh announces the end of World War I from atop a Fairhope Avenue building in an Armistice Day speech on November 11, 1919. McIntosh served two terms as mayor after moving to Fairhope in 1917 and helped organize the Bank of Fairhope. (Courtesy Flora Maye Simmons.)

During the Victory Day parade downtown, residents waved flags, and vehicles, even the community rail car, were decorated with banners to celebrate the end of the war in which many Fairhope residents served. In the background is the Pinequat Shop, operated by the Call family. (Courtesy Marietta Johnson Museum.)

Fairhope, which still takes community pride in being a patriotic town, hosted the state convention of the American Legion in 1939. Here a parade marches down Fairhope Avenue, which was decorated and flying American flags in honor of the occasion. Some spectators watch from the top of a building at right. (Courtesy Ken Niemeyer.)

Only in Fairhope would most of the town turn out to watch a Shakespeare production where local actors would strut their moment on the stage—or in a gully, the town's natural amphitheater. The town held a dozen annual Shakespeare festivals, mostly during the 1920s, in honor of the English bard's birthday. (Courtesy Marietta Johnson Museum.)

These fair ladies from Fairhope starred and sang in *The Taming of the Shrew*, presented in this outdoors setting in April 1929. The plays were produced and directed by Sarah Willard Hiestand, who had lectured and written textbooks on Shakespeare for Chicago schools before retiring with her husband to Fairhope. (Courtesy Warren Stearns.)

This Shakespearian thespian strikes a confident pose after a production. A critic of the day noted, "Some particular and precious spark is generated when neighbors come together to celebrate with dance and song and acting . . . some greatness." (Courtesy Marietta Johnson Museum.)

An old footbridge across one of the town's gullies serves as a dramatic backdrop for this sword-fight scene by two Shakespeare Festival players. There was no admission charge to the plays, which were presented as a gift. The productions also drew large audiences, including high school classes, from over the bay in Mobile. (Courtesy Claire Totten Gray.)

May Day was a special occasion every year when a queen was selected from lovely representatives of surrounding communities to preside over a court that gathered at May Day Park in Daphne, Fairhope's neighboring town. Not infrequently a Fairhope beauty was awarded the honor at the annual observance that began at Daphne Normal School. (Courtesy Flora Maye Simmons.)

In the mid-1930s, the May Queen was Flora Maye Godard of Fairhope (third from left on the last row). Born in 1918, she has kept Fairhope's past and history alive with generous donations of her time and talents. She was a founder of the Fairhope Historical Museum, which contains artifacts, antiques, and historic photographs and documents she preserved.

Every Labor Day, bathing beauties strolled along the pier in an annual beauty contest. The contestants gathered crowds of onlookers as they competed for the coveted title of Miss Labor Day. In 1929, the Miss Fairhope winner was Gladys Grimes, who daintily models a swimming suit fashionable for the time. (Courtesy Bob Mannich.)

Drama and theater were part of life in Fairhope, even for the young. Students at the School of Organic Education take to ladders to paint scenery and hang backdrops for a play at the school, where part of the educational process was learning by doing. Today the Young Players produce annual shows at Theatre 98. (Courtesy Marietta Johnson Museum.)

Comings Hall, on the Organic School campus at the corner of Fairhope Avenue and Bancroft Street, was the setting for many early theatrical productions. These Organic School students were in the cast of *The Man Who Married a Dumb Wife*, first produced in 1915. (Courtesy Marietta Johnson Museum.)

112

Young students at the Fairhope Public School turned out in style for a school play set in an outdoor sylvan scene. The title has been forgotten, but a prince and princess appear to have the lead in a fanciful tale featuring a cast of boys wearing homemade beards and girls in headdresses. (Courtesy Robert Berglin.)

The play *Life with Father,* hot off Broadway, opened the 1947 Fairhope Little Theater season, directed by King Benton. Actors, from left to right, were Felix Bigby, Dan Benton, Ruby Eason, Helen Wilson (with her back to the camera), Dr. Andre Dacovich, Katie Myers, Vance Mason, and Bill Bell. (Courtesy Bill Bell.)

Fairhope Avenue was the scene of parades and local celebrations. Here Arthur Fairhope "Spider" Gaston and Helen Call, two of the first children born to single-taxer settlers after they arrived, are honored in 1958 during the town's Golden Jubilee celebration of its incorporation as a municipality 50 years earlier. (Courtesy Rusty Godard.)

Ten

FORGOTTEN FAIRHOPE

Here the streets of Fairhope were like none of the streets when she was a child
and they would visit—all these homes had sprung up since then,
none of the old waterfront homes survived, long gone, she had long ago mourned them
and now their own ghosts lay over the newer homes like veils, or mosquito netting.

—Brad Watson, "A Lost Paradise," from *The Heaven of Mercury,*
2003 National Book Award nominee

Ladies in white dresses on Fairhope's waterfront in 1912 are a reminder of sweeter times and simpler pleasures on the Eastern Shore. The shore is famed for a rare phenomenon called Jubilee, where fish, crab, shrimp, and other sea life come to the shallows in certain weather conditions. At the cry of "Jubilee!" everyone grabs a net and heads to the bay. (Courtesy Palmer Hamilton.)

Volunteers work on building another pier house on the bay. Many waterfront homes and several streets, like Orange, Pier, and White, that end at the public park along the bay have their own piers. The rustic wooden public piers are used by boaters, swimmers, fishing parties, and for watching sunsets. (Courtesy FSTC.)

"Beyond the hotel, piers ran from the old summer homes out over the bay. Most of them had a pier house or a handmade lean-to at the end, so a family could sit out on summer nights," wrote author and former Fairhope resident Mark Childress in his 1988 novel *V for Victor*, which was set in the area. (Courtesy Fairhope Historical Museum.)

In Fairhope, which features the Marietta Johnson Botanical Garden downtown, gardens have always been the pride of many of their owners, who have created lush, private backyard retreats. Here Mr. and Mrs. Summner are preparing to plant a palm behind their cottage on Bayview Avenue in the early part of the century. (Courtesy Pinky Bass.)

At the Snug Harbor guesthouse that once stood on Magnolia Avenue, the owners proudly tend their fruit trees. Many of the towering trees lining Fairhope's streets were planted in the early 20th century, when residents were given a financial incentive of 25¢ for every water oak tree they planted. (Courtesy Pinky Bass.)

Originally a Baptist church, the former St. James Episcopal Church building served the congregation from 1920 to 1994 and is now the University of South Alabama auditorium on its Fairhope campus. Here Stephen Riggs and Aline Stapleton emerge from the church after their 1940s wedding. To the right is best man Curtis Willard. (Courtesy Aline Stapleton Riggs.)

Weddings were social events where everyone in town was welcomed. These bridesmaids dressed in elegant attire with matching slippers were attendants at a Fairhope wedding at the beginning of the 20th century. Seated is Anna Linder Anderson, and standing is Gudren Erickson Swanson. (Courtesy Pinky Bass.)

These graceful dancing girls, students at the School of Organic Education, look like playful wood nymphs while performing a dance among a backdrop of pines. Outdoor activity has always been a part of the lifestyle in Fairhope, where today there are street dances and concerts on the bluff. (Courtesy Marietta Johnson Museum.)

The wooden bridge on South Bayview Avenue across Stack's Gully facilitated movement across the town, which grew up along a shoreline interspersed by deep ravines. Early on, this main gully was cleared for public use, but later kudzu, that irrepressible vine planted across the South, was used to stop erosion in the gullies and along the bluffs.

This romantic footbridge across the duck pond at the Fairhope Municipal Park on the bay has been replaced by a newer one, but it is still an inviting spot for weddings, picnics, and feeding the waterfowl. The area also now features the Beach Park Tree Trail, which identifies trees, including two state champions—swamp tupelo and hazel alder. (Courtesy Reed Myers.)

Fairhope has several state champion trees, including a flowering crepe myrtle in the heart of downtown. This view of a woman admiring a beautiful dogwood shows why the New Year's 1895 issue of the *Fairhope Courier* reported the village site was "one of the most beautiful and desirable spots along the whole Eastern Shore of Mobile Bay." (Courtesy Claire Gray.)

Neighbors linger to visit on a leisurely walk along North Bayview Avenue. Residents carried lanterns on their promenades in the evenings in the years before the town got streetlights. These landmark homes are still standing on the east side of Bayview in the first block off Magnolia Avenue. (Courtesy Barbara Beaty.)

The side-wheeler *Apollo*, with room for 540 passengers, arrives at the Fairhope pier. In 1912, local private investors purchased the steamer in New York to make the run across the bay to Mobile and back. Founders selected the waterfront site to provide a good trading and shipping point. Even then, times were changing, with sailing vessels being used mostly for fishing. (Courtesy Barbara Beaty.)

Rathje's store on the left, in this view looking east on Fairhope Avenue, issued its own metal scrip, which was used in exchange for goods. This new general store, built in 1914 to replace the earlier wooden structure next door, sold a bit of everything, including violin string. The building still stands at 331 Fairhope Avenue. (Courtesy Cathy Donelson.)

Hurricanes were and are a potent force and fact of life on the coast. The hurricanes of 1906 and 1916 were particularly destructive in Fairhope, destroying steamers and boats and knocking houses off their foundations. Afterward house-raising crews gathered to help repair buildings and barns hard hit by the high winds. (Courtesy FSTC.)

Satsuma oranges were a tasty citrus treat, and most Fairhope home sites had a fruit tree in the yard. Many farmers were members of the Citrus Growers Association, and Fairhope shipped tons of the fruit by boat and rail to other areas of the country in crates made at the local sawmill. Residents also sent fruit to Northern friends. (Courtesy Reed Myers.)

Leisure hours in Fairhope were often passed in simple pursuits like spending time with family on the front porch. Here three generations of Sundbergs and Slossons gather at the Columns at the corner of Magnolia and Bayview Avenues. Fairhope once was a town of porches, and many homes had sleeping porches across the back. (Courtesy Pinky Bass.)

Children roamed the bay front and played in the streets and gullies unsupervised in the days when everyone knew everyone else in the village. They walked and ran everywhere, and some rode, like young Philip Swift on his pet donkey. (Courtesy Harriet Swift.)

Cars became a fixture on Fairhope streets after the bay boats started catering to automobile traffic, landing vehicles on the pier. Visitors brought cars by boat until the causeway was built across Mobile Bay in 1926 and the steamers stopped running to Fairhope. Here the Sundberg family heads out for a swim in the family car, which displays a Fairhope pendant. (Courtesy Pinky Bass.)

Cheerleaders encouraged the teams at schools in Fairhope, which had its own brand of boosterism. In a 1926 article about the new high school, the Mobile newspaper reported, "Fairhope claims to be the most cosmopolitan village in the world, attracting people of intelligence and progressive thought, as the pole attracts the needle of the compass." (Courtesy Marietta Johnson Museum.)

Despite its modest beginnings, Fairhope was always fashionable. Here Lois Slosson Sundberg poses in a striking black ensemble complete with picture hat. She was pictured earlier with her school students. Fairhopers were well traveled, and visitors also brought the latest styles to town. (Courtesy Pinky Bass.)

Life in the reformist town had its lighter moments. Here John W. Ettel, a New Yorker and Socialist for whom Ettel Street is named, dressed down on purpose. He jokingly posed for this photograph to send to a friend to show him how hard his wife was making him work in Fairhope. (Courtesy Pinky Bass.)

Time has erased the purpose of this somber gathering in a clearing. Perhaps it was to honor the gentleman seated in the foreground? The group surely included members of many organizations listed in the 1915 town directory, such as the Equal Suffrage Association and the Fairhope Socialist Local, which met on Friday nights at the country club, of all places. (Courtesy Rusty Godard.)

An older Ellen Hill lived for over half a century at Sea Cliff, where her cabin became a mecca for tourists who enjoyed her stories of the "old days." She liked to sit on her porch, knitting lovely rugs and watching the ships in the bay, until her death in 1920. (Courtesy Bill Payne.)

Lavigne Berglin and friend display a prize alligator gar caught in 1914. As Fannie Flagg wrote in *Fried Green Tomatoes at the Whistle Stop Café*, written in Fairhope: "P. S. If any of you ever get to Fairhope, Alabama, look us up. I'll be the one sitting on the back porch, cleaning all the fish." (Courtesy Robert Berglin.)